This Is Our Faith

This Is
Our Faith

a guide to life and belief for
Anglicans with a revised chapter
on worship

Ian Stuchbery

Anglican Book Centre
Toronto, Canada

Copyright © 1990
Anglican Book Centre
600 Jarvis Street
Toronto, Ontario
Canada M4Y 2J6

Canadian Cataloguing in Publication Data

Stuchbery, Ian
  This is our faith

Rev. ed.
ISBN 0-921846-21-5

1. Anglican Communion. 2. Anglican Communion –
Prayer-books and devotions – English. I. Title.

BX5614.S88 1990   283   C90-093349-6

Contents

Preface

For a long time, I have been looking unsuccessfully for a simple, one-volume book that I could recommend to people as an introduction to the Christian faith and the Anglican Church. I have in mind inquirers who range from people who come in off the street, to those in an adult confirmation class. It should also serve those people who have been coming to church for years, yet still have only a hazy idea of what the Anglican faith is all about. I wanted such a book to be short enough to fit between the covers of a paperback, but comprehensive enough to cover the broad spectrum of all those things a Christian ought to know.

Of necessity, this present volume is concise and general. However, I do hope that it will go some way toward meeting the needs of a great many people who want to get an overview of the Christian faith and that particular part of the church called the Anglican Communion.

I would hope that those who read this will be stimulated to go on to further, more extensive reading. For that reason, I have included a bibliography of books which will carry on where I have left off. In this respect, I am particularly happy to greet the publication of the series on "The Faith of the Church" by the Episcopal Church in the United States.

My thanks are particularly due to those who have encouraged and helped me in writing this volume — to my family for their patience in demands for silence in a busy home, to Judy Bjerring who typed the final draft, and to my congregation who allowed me to write it in the midst of a busy parish schedule.

"What is a Christian?"

Some years ago, I used to put this question to parents who wanted their children baptised. Their answers were remarkably revealing: "Well, a Christian's someone who's decent and honest — someone who tries to live a good life and be nice to other people!" One of them would go on to suggest: "Of course, you don't need to go to church to be a Christian . . . good Jews and Buddhists are Christian if they live good lives!"

I repeat these struggling attempts to find an answer because I want to show how far most people are from being able to define what "being a Christian" really means. It is important to be clear about our definition, so I will start by examining some of the things that Christianity does *not* mean.

Despite the well-intentioned answers mentioned above, being a Christian does not mean just "being good." There are millions of reasonably good people in the world, and probably more than half of them are not even nominally Christian. "Being good" is an inadequate description of a Christian; how good do we have to be to qualify? Must we be totally good (a saint), in which case none of us would get beyond first base, or should we just be well-intentioned? Simply being good ceases to have any meaning. Similarly, performing the right rituals — going to church twice on Sundays, confessing every week, or reading the Bible every day — also does not make us Christians. No doubt these are things that would be of great help to us in trying to lead Christian lives, but in themselves, they do not make us Christians.

Nor does being born into a Christian society or even a Christian family necessarily make us Christians. Hundreds of thousands of Canadians have been born into a so-called Christian society and grown up in homes which were nominally Anglican, Roman Catholic, or United Church, but the mere accident of their nationality and upbringing does not mean they are Christians.

What, then, is a Christian? The answer is surprisingly simple, and it is found in the baptismal service of the Anglican Prayer Book. (It does not matter whether we look in the traditional Prayer Book or the more modern versions of the baptism service, because what we are looking for is in all of them.)

Look first at the questions that the candidates (or their parents) have to answer. In essence they are threefold, but all three centre upon one crucial point. The candidates have to affirm, first, that they renounce all evil; second, that they believe in the Gospel (as expressed in the historic creeds), and third, that they will commit themselves to Jesus Christ.[1] The ultimate focus of all these questions is the last one. Becoming a Christian means believing in and committing oneself to Jesus Christ — making him the centre of one's life, and seeking always to follow his way rather than one's own.

This is the first thing that "being a Christian" means — to follow Jesus. But there is a second and equally important component. Simply committing myself to follow Jesus is not enough. It sounds all very fine and noble, until I seriously try to do it. Then I fall flat on my face, for alone I do not have sufficient resources. The strength and discipline I require in order to follow Jesus is simply beyond me. Yet many Christians have imagined that this approach is what Christianity is all about. They have built it up into a great and impressive way of life based upon duty and morality. "The Christian is called to follow the path that Jesus trod," they say, and the result is a stern religion of duty and sacrifice. Our problem is that we simply cannot make our Christian journey alone.

To meet this very basic human need, there is a second component to being a Christian — the gift of the new life of the Holy Spirit. And so the sacrament of baptism is not only about our commitment to Jesus, it is also about God's promise to us, the gift of his Holy Spirit. In the prayer preceding baptism, the priest asks that the candidate receive the gift of the Holy Spirit. The subsequent act of signing with the cross has its roots in the ancient symbolism of anointing, in which was signified the pouring out of the Holy Spirit upon the new Christian. In baptism, then, the question, What is a Christian? is answered. *A*

Christian is someone who has committed himself to Christ and has been empowered with the Holy Spirit — the gift of God's own life — to enable him to follow the way of Christ. This is where the Christian faith begins.

What Is Man?

Let us pause for a moment, however, and go back to an even more basic question. What do we really understand by the word *man*? (Here I am not using the word in its sexist sense.) Scientists will naturally answer this question in the only way their discipline will allow. Modern science, of course, has built itself upon the basic assumption that it can only address itself to what can be physically measured. While not denying any other aspect of reality, science can therefore only speak with real authority in the realm of the physical. Thus a scientist will describe a human being in terms of flesh and blood (or if you prefer it, of molecules and atoms).

Yet Christianity has a richer understanding of man, one that grows directly out of the Jewish tradition expressed in the Old Testament. As Christians, we believe the Old Testament is not merely a historical book telling us what certain people believed at various points in history; we believe it actually speaks with authority as the Word of God. And so we take very seriously what it has to tell us about the nature of man.

Now that picture is not totally clear — at least, we do not get the kind of analytical statement that some of us in the twentieth century would much prefer! But the Old Testament is very clear about some things, and from these we can build up a model of what we understand by "man." (We do this in the same way that physicists have built up a working model of the atom.) This model can then be used as a means of further understanding mankind's problem and God's solution to it in Jesus Christ.

The basic biblical material for our understanding of man and his predicament is to be found in the creation stories of Genesis 1 and 2, followed by the story of the fall of man from his ideal relationship with God. The picture of man that emerges from these stories is relatively simple.

Man is, in essence, *a spiritual being*. We must not forget that the modern denial of the world of *spirit* is very recent. Although this denial is a byproduct of scientific thinking, science in no way demands it. Scientists came to an agreement more than a hundred years ago that, within their own discipline, they could only study and pass judgement on the physical world around them. As scientists, they could not deny the reality of another world or dimension of reality called "spirit"; they simply pointed out that it could not be studied by the methods of science. Others certainly went on to deny the spiritual dimension, and our modern technological society has for all practical purposes turned its back on such realms. However, most people have not totally accepted this rejection, and we have recently seen a great revival of interest in spiritual matters, even if this interest has sometimes taken the bizarre form of magic or the occult.

As far as the Christian faith is concerned, this spiritual dimension exists; one of the Bible's fundamental assertions is that man is a *spiritual* being. (Genesis 1.27 says that God created man "in His own image.") At the very centre of our being we are each a soul, and we are set at the meeting point of two worlds: the world of spirit and the world of physical matter. As souls, we are open to these two realities, and each of them penetrates us. In one sense we are physical, made of flesh, blood, and bones; we can be seen, touched, smelled, and measured. We are the object of the physicist's science and an anthropologist's study. We are one animal in a world of many, and our behaviour is conditioned by many of the same things that influence the behaviour of other species.

In another sense we are spiritual, open to the forces and realities of that world. We find these forces described in such diverse sources as the Book of Revelation, the writings of the mystics, and the works of the psychologist C. G. Jung. It is a world to which we in the West have become virtually dead over the last several hundred years.

At the meeting-place of these two worlds, penetrating and being penetrated by both, each of us is a soul, unique and individual. This is the core, the "I" whom God loves and who is capable of responding to that divine love. This core, this human soul, is self-conscious and capable of being open to God through both the spiritual and physical dimensions of God's creation.

But all is not sweetness and light. Within the physical and the spiritual realms are powers of both creativity and destructiveness, of good and evil. Each one of us is placed in this great cosmic setting. But the biblical story of the fall of man takes it even further. Within each of us there is an innate tendency to turn in upon ourselves, and to be corrupted and destroyed by the power of evil that is in creation. (This is the meaning of the story of Adam and Eve in Genesis 3.) This fatal tendency the Jews called *sin*. It stands for the innate selfishness that each one of us knows only too well in our own personalities; and it is this flaw that gets between God and us, separating us from him, from each other, and even from ourselves. Each of us is, in a true sense, a disintegrated person needing to be re-integrated or made whole.

The following diagram might help to indicate what we could call the human predicament.

God's will is for each of us to be at one with him, to enjoy his love, and to respond to him of our own free will.

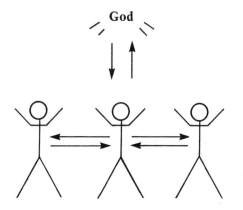

At one with God
and
each other.
Freely responding to
God and each other.

The "fall" indicates our present situation, separated from each other and from God through sin.

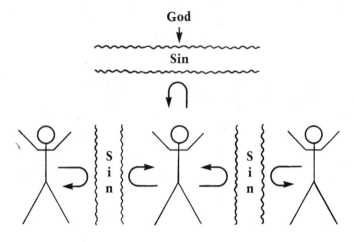

As a result of this sin, the human soul is left vulnerable to the self-centred forces within us and to the power of evil from without. Traditionally, these self-centred forces have been assigned three terms: (1) the emotions, (2) the intellect, and (3) the will. Cut off from God, these centres in the soul take control of us, and we become their slaves. Each of us is, of course, unique, and the degree to which we can be dominated by these three forces is different. There will be times when we are ruled by our *will*; our religion may, for example, become a matter of rules and regulations, expressing our deep conviction that we can live by the strength of our will-power. In some of us, the *emotions* will dominate, and the constant chasing of emotional satisfaction will be our way of life. We see a great deal of this in contemporary North American culture, where acquisitiveness and sensual satisfaction are encouraged by almost every ad on television. Some of us will let the *intellectual* forces predominate; we will try to fulfill ourselves, and give meaning to our lives by acquiring superior knowledge and cultivating the rational side of our personality. Our religion, if we have any, will be cold and detached — an object of study and analysis. In none of these ways of life — the wilful, the emotional or the intellectual — will God really be allowed to live. This is the ultimate victory of sin.

The Good News of Christ

This is the human predicament: man, a unique soul, living at the junction of the spiritual and the physical, is cut off by sin from God, and left at the mercy of the self-centred powers within the depths of his own soul. But it is not God's will or intention that we should live in alienation and suffering. He does not wish us to be dominated and suffocated by our own selfishness, nor does he want us to be victims of the undoubted power of sin and destructiveness in both the physical and spiritual dimensions which we inhabit.

On the other hand, it *is* his will that this state of things should be changed. The Bible puts it in this way: St Paul says that we need "saving" (see especially Romans 5), and this is precisely what the good news of the Gospel is all about. It tells us what *God* has already done to remedy the situation, and it describes what *we* can do appropriate this remedy.

We have come full circle, for the good news is that we can be restored to God and to wholeness by committing ourselves to Christ and by allowing his Holy Spirit to flow into and change our lives. This is what baptism is all about, and it also explains what it means to become a Christian.

In the chapters that follow, I shall assume that we are now at a stage when we have accepted Jesus Christ as Saviour, we have made a definite act of commitment to follow him and make him the centre of our life. I shall also assume that we have invited the Holy Spirit to enter into our life with his new life, so that we may experience his power and be transformed more and more into the people that God is making us to be.

This book is divided into two parts, the first a kind of primer to the Christian life and the second a background study of the Christian faith. I think it is more important to start with what it takes to *live* the Christian life, than to reflect upon its background. In the first part we shall be taking a look at the various components of the Christian life. It is my hope that the reader will be able to put many of the suggestions into effect as we try to be more open to the guidance and power of the Spirit within us. We begin with an all-important chapter on the life of prayer, because I find it difficult to imagine any degree of spiritual life that is not rooted and grounded in regular prayer. There follows a chapter on the sacramental life, explaining the meaning of the sacraments of the church and suggesting ways in which they can enrich our lives. Chapter 4 not only describes the Book of Common Prayer, but is intended to help us find our way around it so that we can use the great amount of useful material it contains. Finally, Chapter 5 suggests ways in which our life-style should not only be rooted in prayer and sacrament, but also expressed in loving our neighbour and being effective agents for Christian change in today's world.

In the second part we will examine the sources of our faith in the Old Testament and in the life of Jesus; we shall see how Christians have tried to explain this faith, and how it has been passed down through the centuries to our own day. Chapter 12 will describe how the Anglican Church of Canada is organized. Finally, I shall deal in an appendix with a number of questions that people frequently ask, under the title of "Questions."

Such a vast scope for such a small book is, I know, courting the criticism of both superficiality and generalization. However, I do hope that it will serve as both an introduction to being a Christian in the Anglican Church of Canada and also as a stimulus to continued reading.

Living
the
Christian
Life

1

A Life of Prayer

Let us begin by asking ourselves a question: what exactly is *prayer*? A dozen different people will come up with as many answers. For some, prayer refers to what Christopher Robin did at the foot of his bed, something infantile that we left behind years ago. At the other end of the spectrum some people may have a mental picture of a Russian mystic or an oriental monk, struggling to pray well after years of self-discipline and training. Is prayer so childish that we are too old and sophisticated for it, or so profound and mysterious that only the most dedicated should even attempt it? Of course, it is neither of these. Prayer is appropriate for every Christian at whatever age or stage of growth in the faith. It is difficult even to think of a person as a Christian unless regular prayer plays some part in his daily life.

What, then, is prayer? It might help to begin by looking at some of our beliefs about God and man. One of the basic assumptions shared by all Christians is that God is *personal*, that he loves and cares for us and is willing to communicate with us. The fundamental assertion of Christianity is that God cares for us so much that he sent his only Son to make possible a new relationship between himself and us. He wants us to know him; he wants us to grow in that relationship.

When any two ordinary people want to get to know each other better and build up a relationship, they normally do it through conversation, listening and speaking to one another. Whoever heard of two would-be friends who turned their backs on each other, ignored each other, and never spoke? Conversation is the natural way to grow near to someone, the way we slowly grow in trust and ultimately come to care for and love another person.

It is just like this with God — and the name we give to this two-way conversation is *prayer*. It is the way, above all others, in which we come to know God as person, and let him guide and transform our lives.

But first, before we look at some of the forms that prayer can take, here are some very down-to-earth hints about how to begin in our prayer life, how to start again after many years off the job! It should go without saying that the most obvious way to begin praying is to pray, not just to talk or read about it! But it is at precisely this point that many of us get stuck, simply because we have not dealt with some obstacles that appear right at the start. Let us face them now.

How often should I pray? Certainly, at least once every day. We should no more think of going without a prayer time each day than we should think of neglecting food, drink, or sleep. If we do, we become spiritually stunted, and God remains little more than a remote possibility. We do not have to spend hours each day in prayer; we are not all called upon to be monks or nuns. But a day should not go by without a time of prayer.

When should we pray, and for how long? There are no absolute rules about this. The answers will be determined by a variety of things, ranging from our body's metabolism and our work patterns to the availability of the privacy, which is necessary if we are to pray properly. We need to plan our time carefully. This raises the question of "how long?" I am not talking here of what are often called "arrow prayers" or snatched times of prayer on the subway or driving to the office. I am talking of a period of time when we can be alone, silent, and relaxed — ready to be with God and open to him. Such a period may be as short as ten minutes, although it will be much more valuable if we make it longer.

When can we fence off such time? Where can we do it? We have to decide these answers deliberately. For one person, it may be in the early morning. I have a busy friend who has little time during the day to be quiet, but he is a natural early riser; each day he spends from 6 A.M. to 7 A.M. alone with God, in the sitting-room, before anyone else is around to disturb him. If we are gifted with such a metabolism, then this is probably the best possible time. For others, the best opportunity may be later in the evening. A husband and wife may find a time when they can each pray silently (perhaps with each other) at the end of the day in the privacy of their bedroom. Some people may slip into a downtown church for half an hour at noonday; a parish priest may spend the first part of the day quietly before the altar in the church; a housewife might find time to be alone immediately after the last child has left for school, before facing the daily chores. There are many times and places. The important thing is to plan the workable ones for ourselves — and then make sure we use them well!

So far, so good. I am resolved to spend twenty minutes each morning with God at 9.00 A.M. in the sitting-room. But how do I go about it when the time comes? Many of us have surely experienced our firm resolution slowly slipping away as we spend that twenty minutes wondering what on earth we should be doing! So we say an *Our Father*, rattle off a prayer that we have known since childhood, string a few requests together, and then come to an abrupt end, feeling vaguely that we have wasted the time. And indeed we have, simply because we have not laid down some simple guidelines as to what we might do and how we might go about it. We need to be clear about two basic matters: (a) what kinds of prayer we use, and (b) how we are going to include them in our prayer time. Then our prayers will consist of a "balanced diet" and so keep us prayerfully healthy.

Vocal Prayer

We return to our image of prayer as our conversation with God. Any healthy dialogue is a two-way affair. It is exactly the same in our prayer with God. The prayers we *speak* to God are usually described as vocal prayer.

For most of us, speaking *to* God is what we usually mean when we talk about prayer. In fact, we actually use the phrase "saying our prayers" — and often we do not progress beyond that stage. As in normal conversation, most of us are far more concerned about being heard than we are about listening to what the other person has to say. So most of us begin our prayer experience by talking to God. For nearly all of us, that means asking God for what we want. We need to learn how our vocal prayer can grow from a childish "give me" level to something richer and more mature. What are the ingredients of healthy vocal prayer?

A useful clue is given to us in chapter 6 of the Book of Isaiah. It describes a deeply religious experience by which the prophet was called to follow God. It is worth noting the progression of the experience. At first Isaiah reacted with awe and wonder to this shattering vision. We can picture him falling on his face in *adoration*. Then he became aware of his complete unworthiness and sin. He felt unfit to remain in the presence of God — and he blurted out these words of *confession*: "Woe is me, for I am a man of unclean lips." The Lord then sent an angel with a live coal from the altar. When the angel touched Isaiah with the coal he was forgiven and cleansed. We can imagine his overwhelming sense of *thanksgiving* as his sin was purged.

In this story we have a vivid portrayal of the first three ingredients of vocal prayer: adoration, confession, and thanksgiving. If we add only two more ingredients, we have a very simple framework upon which to construct this part of our prayer time with God. The five elements contained in any healthy vocal prayer form the easily remembered word PACTS:

| Pause | Adore | Confess | Thank | Supplicate |

1 Pause. We shall consider this preparatory stage of prayer later, when we come to look at how we listen to God. Without a pause at the beginning of any prayer time, we shall not be in a sufficiently relaxed state of mind either to speak or listen properly to God.

2 Adoration. This is probably the most neglected part of prayer; I believe it is also one of the most important parts. Time and again, when I have forgotten or been in too much of a hurry for it, the resulting prayer time has been lifeless and uncreative. I am sure this is not a coincidence. What is adoration? Simply telling God how wonderful he is, and conveying that we love him. This, after all, is what worship is really all about: telling God what he is "worth." If it is important for me to tell the members of my family that I love them, then it is much more important for me to say this to God! After all, has he not made me, so that I am able to enjoy this amazing life, and has he not given me the gift of his eternal life, so that I may live eternally? Does that not deserve a word of recognition and praise? If Isaiah fell on his face in awe before the majesty of God, should I not glorify God for bestowing love and mercy on me?

But how do we say these things if we are not very good at adoration. Try praising God for a few minutes — it is astonishing how rapidly we run out of words and expressions! Those who have experienced a renewed presence of the Holy Spirit and perhaps are able to pray or sing through the gift of tongues will know the immense value of such gifts in enabling us to praise God. But I still believe that we need to make the most of the many prayers of adoration that have been handed down to us from the past. And here I am going to suggest a very practical aid to our prayers. Right from the start, we need to buy a small, loose-leaf book and create our own personal prayer book. We can then have this notebook beside us whenever we settle down to pray, and it can be of enormous benefit in helping us to make maximum use of the time at our disposal. Every hour spent putting it together will be rewarded by hundreds of hours saved when we use it in our daily prayers.

We would begin by reserving a large part of this book for vocal prayers, with separate sections for each "ingredient." Under *adoration* we might copy out some classic prayers of praise from a variety of prayer anthologies which we can find in any religious bookstore. We can also copy out particular verses of praise from the Bible,[2] especially from the epistles and the Book of Revelation. Above all, we can note those psalms of praise that most appeal to us. Psalms 104 and 145-150 in particular are superb examples of adoration prayers which have inspired men and women for several thousand years. Such a personal collection will be invaluable and will supplement the more spontaneous words of praise which should be a part of any time of adoration.

3 Confession. Later on, I shall describe the act of sacramental confession and how to prepare for it. But confession should not be just an occasional stock-taking of how we stand with God; it should be part of our regular daily prayer. We may undertake a thorough house-cleaning less frequently and use a more rigorous form of self-examination then, but each day we need to "come clean" before God and offer up our backslidings to him. If we do this every day, we shall be less liable to have false impressions about ourselves, and be better able to deal with our sins and weaknesses before they have time to get a strong hold on us. We do not necessarily need to use a particular form of self-examination. If we pray to God to "float" our sins up to the surface of the mind, we shall realize our transgressions against him, others, and ourselves. And all we need to do is admit them, simply and without fuss. No special form of confession is needed. We just tell God where we have done wrong, resolve not to do it again, ask his forgiveness, and pray for the strength to resist the temptation when it comes again.

4 Thanksgiving. So often, we seem to take God too much for granted; it never occurs to us that we should ever thank him. Life goes on more or less happily, day by day, and we assume that it will continue to do so. We are less aware of our blessings than we are of the occasional bad times, which we ask God to help us through. I remember visiting a woman in hospital years ago, and all she could do was tell me the problems her sickness was causing in her family. I was tempted to go along with her self-pity until I suddenly realized that, in the same terrace of houses where she was living, there were several families facing difficulties at least as great as hers. In fact, there were more people in that block who had serious problems than those who did not. Instead of wondering why a particular disaster happens, we should be thanking God that things are going so well.

It also happens that some people can become overly bowed down with a sense of their own sinfulness, and seem to know little of the joy of being a Christian. Although this attitude may stem from a depressive tendency, I have often found that such a person rarely takes the trouble to *thank* God during times of prayer. Yet when we thank God, deliberately and regularly, we have a powerful antidote to this particular spiritual fault.

Thanking God may be done spontaneously — this will, of course, come more easily with practice — but we can also give ourselves some help by using our personal notebook. Copy out some classic prayers of thanks which seem particularly helpful. We may want to compose one for personal use, leaving room in it to add particular things for which we shall want to thank God. It is also useful to think of a few hooks on which we might hang some particular "thank you's" in our daily prayer time. Here are some examples:

— the world we live in,
— material things,
— special events,

— people close to us, who love and care for us,

— things we find difficult, yet which help us to grow.

5 Supplication. We end our prayer time with our personal "shopping list." People sometimes say: "But surely it's very selfish to ask God for anything," or "if God knows what we need, then he doesn't need us to ask him?" Yet several times in the Bible our Lord tells us to ask. "Ask and you shall receive" (Luke 11.9), and "when two or three agree about anything and ask it in my name, it shall be given" (Matthew 18.20). Jesus went on to assure his followers that none of their prayers would go unheard: "Everyone who asks shall receive, and anyone who seeks shall find and the door will be opened to him who knocks. Would any of you who are fathers give your son a stone when he asks for bread? Or would you give him a snake when he asks for a fish. Bad as you are, you know how to give good things to your children. How much more, then, will your Father in heaven give good things to those who ask him" (Matthew 7.8–11). Why does God wish us to ask him for what we need? There is no simple answer to this. I suspect that it is somehow connected with man's freedom, that quality which makes us most human. God never forces himself upon us; he always respects our human freedom. For that reason, perhaps, he waits for us to invite him into our lives to deal with a particular situation.

How should we go about asking? First of all, it helps to divide our requests between those for others and those for ourselves. Even then, it is not easy to know where to begin or end! We need a balance between laziness (not bothering to pray for others) and excessive zeal (having so many things to pray for that we become overloaded). It will help enormously to use this personal notebook to put some kind of order into our *intercessions*, our prayers for others. One way of doing this is by dividing them into three groups:

a People and things we pray for every day:
family, special friends, people who suffer, certain parish needs;

b People and things we pray for once a week:
peace and justice in the world, the church near and far, prisoners, the poor, refugees, those we work with;

c Things that crop up unexpectedly:
   victims of earthquakes, a sudden illness, a newly elected
   government, a couple just married.

In addition, we may have responsibilities as a member of a
prayer team; so we shall want to include those special concerns
on our list. Under each general heading, we might wish to write
lists of *particular* things or people for whom we wish to pray.
Again, we might want to assign the headings to particular days
of the week. We could end up with a pattern that began like this.

Mondays	1	Family, special friends, etc.
		(List of these . . .)
	2	Peace and justice in the world.
		(List of particular examples . . .)
Tuesdays	1	Family, special friends, etc.
		(List of these . . .)
	2	The church.
		Particular areas of the church's life and work, world, diocesan and parish.
Wednesdays	1	Family, etc.
	2	Victims of violence and repression. Particular concerns about refugees, prisoners, the hungry, landless, etc.

The great value of this kind of arrangement is that we can get
down to the actual business of intercession immediately each
day, without having to waste time deciding about our prayer
concerns. The daily plan is adjusted, of course, as new or different prayer needs arise. It is also important that we revise the
overall plan periodically so it does not become too automatic.

A word here about the seriousness with which we should
approach this kind of prayer. We need to be quite clear about
two very important truths. First, intercessory prayer is *real*.
God has promised us that he will hear and respond to our
requests, and he does. I want to emphasize this point as being of
very great importance. I grew up in a church where we often
prayed for other people, but there was never a genuine expectancy that our prayers would be answered —*truly* answered. We
said intercessory prayers because we felt this to be right, but we
never really expected to get results. Since that time, I have had
cause to change my ideas radically because of a new awareness

that God does indeed answer our prayers. However, I am equally convinced that, in order to experience the reality of such prayer, we need to bring to it a spirit of genuine expectancy, firmly believing that God is indeed there, both wanting and able to respond.

Second, it is part of our basic *work* as Christians that we should pray for others. We are called to be professional prayers (praying people) on behalf of God's world. In the Middle Ages, it was considered a special calling for monks and nuns to be the professional prayers on behalf of the rest of the church. They deliberately cloistered themselves in order to get on with the business of praying, without having to be bothered by the demands of ordinary daily life. Yet, no matter how valuable the prayer life of the religious may be in the total life of the church, the duty to pray for others is still the job of every Christian. It is very much our business.

From these two truths, several things follow. Because intercession really does work, we should take it extremely seriously. The writer Martin Thornton tells the story of a priest who, when asked, "Father, please would you pray for John?" replied: "Yes, of course, Mrs. Smith. I see that I haven't got room in my intercessions on Monday or Tuesday, but I will pray for him on Thursday and Friday. Would you like me to include him in next week's intercessions as well?" Whatever else may be said about this reply, it certainly shows that the priest took his job of intercession with business-like efficiency! Similarly, we should pray for people carefully and proficiently.

Finally, in our requests, we come to ourselves. It is not wrong to pray for ourselves. God wants us to grow, to be more loving, to live full, happy, and healthy lives, and there is every reason to pray for these things. Above all, we will find ourselves praying, "Your will be done in me, Lord." We shall want to make him and his will more and more the centre of our lives. He taught us to put his kingdom (his rule) first, and promised that all would follow from there. So, as we mature in prayer, we shall pray less and less for our own narrow concerns, and more and more that the Lord may live in us and direct our lives. Such prayer, applied to each day's events, will spring most naturally from the heart. Nevertheless, it might still be of value to copy out some similar prayers into our notebook.

Quite recently, my parish needed $4,000.00 to pay off the estimated deficit at the year's end. We decided not to have a mini-campaign to bring in the money, but chose simply to pray for it. We did this privately, as well as on three or four Sunday mornings in church. Within the allotted month, $4,019.00 came in, made up of a variety of donations. I was excited when the last contributions arrived, and I went to tell my wife. Instead of the expected "Wow, that's fantastic!" she simply said: "Well, what else did you expect? We prayed for it, didn't we?" Rule number one — prayer is real.

"Listening Prayer" or Meditation

Most of us begin with vocal prayer, but this certainly does not describe the whole of prayer. Just as conversation includes not only talking but also listening, so does prayer. In fact, listening to God is probably even more important than talking to him, yet many of us never get around to it. If we never listen, it is difficult to see how God can ever really influence, let alone transform, our lives. So we need, quite deliberately, to set aside time in our weekly prayer schedule to be quiet and give the Lord the chance to get through to us. If we do, we can be quite sure that he will speak, although it may take some patience and time before we are able to recognize his voice. How, then, can we learn to listen to or meditate upon God?

The word "meditation" has recently been used in a variety of ways, especially with the rise to fashion of the Eastern religions. Meditation usually conjures up images of tough and sustained disciplines which take years to master. These practices are supposed to lead to a mystical breakthrough or enlightenment. Without denying the validity of this kind of experience, I mean something much different. Just as the Christian Gospel assures us that salvation is not the result of our own efforts but the free gift of God (which we have only to accept in faith), so we can be open to the presence of God in meditation, without a lifetime of discipline and effort. We can hear God and know him in our experience very simply, once we have learned the essential truth of accepting him and being open to his Spirit. Meditation to the Christian is a relatively simple matter, and more important, it is for everyone.

Let's return to the question: how do we set about meditating? Again, as with vocal prayer, I will stress the two basic and straightforward steps. First, we need to make time and place in our weekly prayer pattern — anything from a period of daily quiet to perhaps a couple of sessions a week. Second, we need to be prepared for what we are going to do, so that we do not waste most of the time trying to decide. Here is a suggested pattern of how to make a meditation.

1 Spend some minutes in *relaxation*. We need to unwind; we shall never hear God if the circuits of our mind are still buzzing with the agenda of the day. There are several ways we can do this. We clearly need to be quiet and away from distraction. This is certainly not the type of prayer to use on the way to work in a bus! We may use a relaxation technique similar to the one expectant mothers are taught as they prepare for natural childbirth: the simple process of tightening and relaxing each muscle in the body, beginning with the feet and hands, and ending with the head. Such exercises are not unlike some basic yoga practices which were originally developed as a means of preparation for meditation.

One feature of such exercises is the use of controlled deep breathing, which has a deeply calming effect on the human body. Transcendental meditation also makes use of this technique, combining it with a *mantra* or phrase, repeated over and over again. There is nothing particularly profound or mysterious about this method; it has been used for centuries as a means of relaxing the body and the mind so that we can be ready to meditate. In the Christian tradition, certain phrases have commonly been repeated. These have the added effect of focusing the mind on God. The Eastern Orthodox "Jesus Prayer" ("Jesus Christ, Son of God, have mercy") has been used by millions of Christians as a means of relaxing and focusing the mind on Jesus.

Some people also find it useful to fix their eyes on some sacred object, such as a crucifix, a picture, or the Blessed Sacrament, so that the eyes as well as the lips may be similarly engaged with the same purpose. The sense of touch can also be brought into play; the rosary has been used in this way by generations of Catholics. I find it helpful to hold the small crucifix I wear round my neck, as I use my Christian mantra.

It is important to realize two complementary truths about these practices. First of all, a period of unwinding, relaxation, or "centering-in" (to use a phrase of Dr Morton Kelsey's)[3] is absolutely essential if we are to be open to God's voice in meditation. Second, there is nothing magical or mysterious about these practices. Although immensely valuable, they are simply ways to prepare ourselves for the listening which is to follow.

2 When we have sufficiently relaxed, we begin the meditation. Usually, as Christians, we use the Bible as the means to this end. It is, after all, God's word to us through which he has spoken to generations of Christians, and it is logical and true that he speaks through the Bible to us today, often with great and personal force. What follows is a very basic way of listening to God through what he is saying to us in the Bible. It is not the same as Bible study, which is essentially an intellectual pursuit, and equally important in its own right. Rather, it is a devotional use of scripture which seeks not to analyse, but to listen.

a Having decided what to read, glance over the passage fairly quickly, so as to get an immediate feel of what it is all about. This will give a kind of mental framework to guide us.

b Then, read it again, this time much more slowly, letting the impact of the words sink in.

c Imagine the scene. (I am here thinking of an incident rather than a piece of teaching in an epistle). Put yourself into the picture. Identify with one of the characters or speakers. Feel how they felt. Imagine what you would have felt, done, or said. Mull over the scene — enjoy it as you would a great wine or a beautiful landscape. Do not be in a hurry.

d Slowly begin to ask yourself, "What is this saying to me now?" The answer may be more or less intellectual. It may raise a question about something we are worrying about; it may relate to some course of action we were going to embark upon. It may directly parallel something in our immediate experience. Something will inevitably come out of the meditation to quieten or raise our conscience, stimulate our creativity, lead to a deeper understanding of a relationship, heal a hurtful memory, or move us to greater compassion.

God always speaks, although sometimes he does so more directly or insistently than others. We need always to be prayerfully open to him. At first, we may not be aware of him, but hindsight, experience, faithfulness, and sharing with others will always open our eyes.

e When we have listened in this way, we often need to make a deliberate resolution to do (or stop doing) something. This is a useful discipline. It helps sharpen our perception of what has happened; and we can link it to our will, so that our lives really are affected.

f Finally, we close with a prayer of commitment and thanks, ending, perhaps, with the grace.

This is a simple way of opening ourselves to what God has to say to us in our prayers. Obviously there is more to meditation than this very basic form, but I am deliberately limiting myself to this one description. Much could be said about how God speaks to us in meditation, and how this relates to our understanding of human psychology.

Christians also use other methods of opening themselves to God in addition to those which I have just described. There is a whole field of dream experience which is seen by some as a powerful medium through which the Lord speaks to us. These questions have all been explored in a fascinating manner by Dr Morton Kelsey, a Christian teacher who has done much to explain prayer and dream experiences in the light of Jungian psychology and with a deep understanding of the Bible. For both theoretical explanation and very practical guidance, his works are strongly to be recommended by those who would seriously like to develop their prayer life.

Contemplation

Meditation is not to be confused with contemplation, although the two words have frequently been treated as synonyms. Meditation is primarily an activity of the intellect and the imagination, and it is probably for this reason that it has received so much more attention over the past few centuries. In the Western world's preoccupation with what is rational and scientific, it was almost inevitable that attention should be focused on the intellectual side of prayer. This emphasis on the intellect in meditation should have been obvious in the preceding pages. We use our minds analytically and imaginatively to draw out the meaning of the Bible and apply it to our lives.

In contrast, contemplation has very little to do with the intellect. In fact, it demands a deliberate rejection of both the intellect and the emotions. Consequently, in the prayer of contemplation we are not to seek either emotional or intellectual satisfaction; they are deliberately rejected.

What, then, is the aim of contemplative prayer? The answer is fairly simple: its aim is to focus our entire *will* upon God, and nothing else. In contemplation, we do not pray to God in order to produce pleasant feelings or emotions (although this might be one side-effect). Nor do we wish our minds to be somehow edified or fed. We pray to God solely because he is there and he is adorable. It is impossible to stress this aspect too much; in contemplation, we do not expect to gain anything directly. Contemplation consists solely in directing our love, our attention, our will to God . . . and nothing else.

Certainly there are fruits to be gained, but they are not immediately apparent in the form of enlightenment or warm feelings. They will probably be discerned by others long before we notice them in ourselves. The fruit of contemplation is, in fact, our transformation into the likeness of God. As our will, our love, is directed to and concentrated upon God in the most unselfish way possible, so are we most open to all the love and transforming grace which he wants to pour upon us. So, even though the immediate fruits of contemplation are almost undiscernible, in the long run they are the richest.

We have seen what contemplation is and is not, but how do we set about it? In answering this question, I have been helped immensely by a book by Basil Pennington, called *Centering Prayer*.

He describes contemplation as "centering in," a process that has three stages: (1) entry into the prayer; (2) the actual resting in the presence of God, and (3) emerging from the prayer. Underlying all three stages is the image of our Lord "at the centre" of our being, the Divine Self at the very core of our own individual selves. In order to get in touch with the God-at-the-centre, we begin by letting go our attachment to the things around us, calming the busyness of our minds, and concentrating instead on "centering in."

The first stage is very similar to the one I described when writing about meditation. The object is to detach ourselves from the bombardment of stimuli which clutter our minds during our waking hours. So we deliberately relax, using whatever techniques we find most helpful. All the time, our mind concentrates upon what it is we are about to do: we are to focus directly upon God, the all-loving, all-caring, all-powerful God who has revealed himself to us in Jesus and who now lives within us through the indwelling of the Holy Spirit. We are directing ourselves to the heart of pure compassion who deeply wants to return our love and flood us with his infinitely greater life and love.

As we relax and focus our attention upon God, so now we begin to repeat a single word; usually it will be the divine name Jesus or one of his titles, such as Lord or Saviour. What follows is very simple to describe although not so easy to do. We simply keep repeating the name over and over again, all the time keeping our attention focused on God. This is our aim, to let nothing separate us from him. It is an act of pure will, regardless of what our emotions or our intellect may be telling us. And so we persist in repeating the word and endeavouring to keep our attention on God, the sole object of our adoration.

But the mind does not like to be ignored any more than the emotions do, and we will find that our attention will again and again be diverted. Pennington has written at length about the various kinds of diversions and what they represent. These diversions may be very simple and obvious — the noise of a passing car or the anxiety about tomorrow's exam — but they will become more subtle, especially as we "centre in" more deeply. They may take the form of a delightful sensation crying out to be savoured, a fascinating thought that the mind wants to explore, or even a sense of peace in God's presence for which we want to burst into thanks. But none of these is the object of contemplation. In fact, they are like so many lures which distract us from our only true aim — the direction of our full love and will to God alone. The way to resist each one of them is simply to return to the word and the object of our contemplation, to

God alone. This may mean that we have to reject strongly these thoughts and sensations; more often we just have to lay them gently aside and return once more to our word and God.

These are but the bare bones of what this "resting in God's presence" is all about. In reality, it brings us face to face with ourselves "in depth," and it is usually the occasion of much self-knowledge on our way to an encounter with the God within.

The third stage of contemplation is that of emergence, which may be likened to emerging from a dream. We should not do it abruptly but slowly, so that the refreshment of the prayer may flow over into the stream-of-conscious awareness. The best way to do this is by slowing reciting the Lord's Prayer, offering it as an act of thanks for the time we have spent with the Lord. Two or three minutes are certainly not too long to spend in this closing stage.

In ending this section on contemplative prayer, there are two things that I would like to emphasize. First, this is a form of prayer that has been neglected for far too long and, in too many people's minds, left to "advanced pray-ers." This is both sad and nonsensical, because contemplation is a form of prayer for everyone. With the renewed interest in spiritual growth taking place in the church at the moment, contemplation should certainly be encouraged. Second, I must re-emphasize my initial remarks even at the risk of repetition. Contemplation is a prayer neither of the emotions nor of the intellect, but of the will. Unlike some other forms of spiritual activity, we must not judge it by the emotional or intellectual satisfaction that it brings. Its importance lies precisely in that it does not bring these immediate rewards. Of all forms of prayer, it is the highest form of praise we can give to our Father.

Some Problems and Other Matters in Prayer

I have already remarked that one of the primary sources of difficulty in prayer is the business of actually getting down to it, and I have suggested some ways in which we might cope with this problem. However, other difficulties also arise once we have begun. Here are some ways in which they might be overcome.

1   Wandering Thoughts. This constitutes by far the most common obstacle affecting everyone who seriously tries to meditate. It is not difficult to see why, when we relax our minds, our consciousness is immediately bombarded with thoughts which rise to the surface. When we are busy, there is no room in our thoughts for anything that might divert us from our purposes. But, when our concentration on a specific subject ceases, all kinds of things float into our consciousness. As we try to relax into prayer, distractions inevitably arise: we worry about those bothersome thoughts which will not go away, and then our prayer time is destroyed.

The first way to deal with these persistent thoughts is simply to include them in our prayer. If your friend David's bad temper comes into your mind, pray that God will deal with it. If you start worrying about a difficult interview coming up later in the day, hold it up to God and ask him to direct it. If you suddenly remember an appointment, pray that it will go well. Many have found this method useful; the wandering thoughts are dealt with and they go away.

I must admit, however, that this has never worked very well with me. Instead of going away, my prayer time all too easily becomes dominated by more and more thoughts which all need to be prayed about! This may be all very well in itself, but as a way of dispelling such thoughts, it leaves much to be desired! Instead, I have found a second method to be more effective. When you pray, always have a pen and a piece of paper handy. When stray thoughts or anxieties come crowding into the silence, simply jot them down one by one. Usually just a single word or two will do the trick: "Write Mary. Buy bread. Call Toronto. Plan next Tuesday. See John about paper," etc. Once committed to paper, they will go away but not be forgotten, and can be dealt with later in the day. I have found this method to work 90% of the time, and it is well worth the effort it takes to jot the thoughts down.

2   Posture. Should I sit, kneel, stand, or even lie down to pray? An absurd question? Maybe, but it is one that people sometimes ask. In church, of course, we simply do what everyone else does, but on our own, it really does not matter. Some people feel that kneeling helps them get into the right frame of mind. I remember one elderly lady of 104 whom I used to visit; she always insisted on kneeling upright without any support in order to pray! So be it. Others find that sore knees, a stiff back, and a knotted stomach lead to wandering thoughts that simply will not go away. It is interesting to recollect that Gautama Buddha recommended that one should meditate on a reasonably full stomach, while sitting in the lotus or cross-legged position. In other words, the body should be comfortable, yet not so comfortable as to induce sleep! Each of us should discover what posture suits us best, so that we can relax our body and be free to pray.

3 But God Doesn't Speak. The difficulty here is often that we do not know how to hear God. What do we expect — a booming voice out of the dark? The vision of a shining angel? Undoubtedly, the Lord does speak to some of us in such shattering ways — but not very often. More frequently, it is in a quiet low-key way which we may only recognize in retrospect. Occasionally, there will be a clue in the word or phrase we have been meditating on; sometimes there will be a quiet conviction that such and such a course is right for us; we may experience a sense of unusual peace or compassion, perhaps focused upon another person; we may even find ourselves able to do or say something normally beyond our capacity. Occasionally, we shall simply "know" God is there. This kind of conviction is difficult to describe to someone who has never experienced it. Nevertheless, it is important to state that it is not the same "mere emotionalism" sometimes whipped up at a religious meeting, although God certainly uses our emotions to make his presence felt. Regardless of the many ways in which we hear God, two things seem to be true: God is heard only when we open ourselves to him in *faith* (to approach him with a skeptical mind is to be deaf to him); second, the deeper this relationship with God grows, the more we shall get used to hearing his voice or sensing his presence. In other words, persistence pays off!

4 Speaking in Tongues. This is one of those spiritual phenomena that has suddenly come into the forefront as a result of the charismatic movement over the last fifteen or so years. Simply stated, it refers to a kind of vocal prayer language which is not the normal language of the person; it is usually unknown to him or her and, indeed, is usually not a known language at all.

Because so much unwarranted fear seems to have been attached to this phenomenon by those who have not experienced it for themselves, it is important that it be set in its proper context.

First of all, the gift of tongues was one of the signs in the early church that a person had been filled with the Holy Spirit. Read the story of Pentecost in the second chapter of Acts. Saint Paul also refers frequently to the gift in his first letter to the Corinthians. It is completely orthodox, and seems to have appeared in the life of the church whenever there has been an experience of renewal in the Spirit. Speaking in tongues is nothing new and is nothing to be alarmed about. Instead, if we are to accept the New Testament accounts of the Christian life, we should be much more alarmed at the obvious *lack* of the practice in the more recent past. If it is a sign of the Spirit's presence, then we should surely expect and hope for it in our private and corporate prayer life.

But what exactly is speaking in tongues? I do not want to get into any kind of spiritual or psychological analysis here, other than to say that the ability is not related to anything we have previously learned. Instead, there is every reason to accept the biblical truth that it is a gift from God, the object of which seems simply to be that we might praise him in a much freer way than we are normally able. Speaking in tongues seems to take over when all our usual attempts at praise fall short. However, some kind of distinction is necessary at this point. Usually, speaking in tongues is a very personal and private form of praise, most often found in our own private prayer time, and as such, it has a noticeable releasing and renewing effect. Because it usually *is* a private form of prayer and those who practise it are often reluctant to use it in public, many of us are simply unaware of the increasing number of people who have this gift today.

Yet it may also be used corporately. In a prayer-meeting, for example, the whole group may join together in "singing in tongues" to produce a very beautiful form of sung praise (sounding not unlike the amazing "Spem in alium," a forty-part motet by Thomas Tallis!). Providing none are taken by surprise at this sound, such singing can play a very stimulating part in the worship of a group.

Yet another form of speaking in tongues has to do with the gift of prophecy. I said earlier that God rarely speaks to people through a ''voice,'' and this is generally true. Yet a clear exception to this is when he speaks *through* someone who has the gift of prophecy. Again, a word of explanation is needed. This gift has undoubtedly been left dormant in the life of the church for many years (if not centuries), so we have got used to thinking of it only as something that used to happen long ago in the days of the Bible. We greet its presence now with a sense of skepticism and suspicion. If we paid more heed to the New Testament, however, we might realize that it is a gift to be treasured and used.

God sometimes speaks to the Christian community through one of its members who has the gift of prophecy. Such a person feels prompted to convey to the group words that he has not consciously formed, but which he feels he has to share. Inevitably, someone else in the group (if that group is genuinely sensitive to God's presence) will be able to confirm that these words are authentic, usually because the thoughts expressed have been impinging themselves on his mind as well. Very often the original prophecy may be given in a language of tongues (which may even be in a genuine language unknown to the speaker). In such a case, someone will be able to interpret what God is saying to the community.

I realize that this will sound astonishing to those who have not experienced it, but the gift of tongues is thoroughly biblical, and it is present in a large number of church groups and congregations today. It is a subject that obviously demands deeper attention, and fortunately a number of books have been written on the subject in recent years. (Some of these are listed in the bibliography.)

5   Praying with Others. I have written elsewhere[4] of my experience in praying with others, and I explained how the discovery of praying together led to a great leap forward in my own life in Christ. I was meeting with a small study group which one evening decided actually to *pray* rather than just to *talk* about it; soon, many things started to happen in my life. One of the most important lessons I learned was that there is more to prayer than praying in private and taking part in the Sunday morning liturgy of the church. What I learned was the crucial importance of the small prayer group — a group of Christians meeting weekly to share their spiritual lives and grow in prayer together.

In saying this, I do not mean to diminish the value of the discussion or study group that meets regularly in the church or someone's home. This has its own important place in the church, which has a woefully low standard of theological education among its members. But only a *praying* group can help each other to grow in the actual experience of coming to know our Lord and living in the life of his Spirit. I am therefore urging the development of such groups and their use as living aids to our prayer life. What does one do in such groups? These are some simple suggestions for developing mutual prayer.

a Here is a simple group meditation, which might be done in one of two ways.

   1 Someone reads a passage aloud. Then everyone reads their own copy in silence for ten minutes. In that ten minutes, each member makes a note of (i) something that hits him forcefully, (ii) some enlightenment that comes to him, and (iii) any questions that arise. (The "signs" for these three stages might be an exclamation mark, a candle, and a question mark.) Then, going round the circle, he briefly shares these notes. When each has spoken, the floor is open for all to share.

   2 Another approach is to read the passage aloud. Each person makes a snap, "top of head" comment. It is read again, and each member has a chance to share his second thought in the light of what someone else said the first time. It is then read for a third time. Now, comments can be shared only in the form of prayer to God.

b Another kind of group prayer is sometimes called "conversational prayer." The group's prayers quite literally follow the form of a group conversation, only the conversation is all directed to God. Thus, one person picks up where another has left off, extending and developing the theme as one does in a normal conversation. Alternatively, someone may change the subject or switch from thanksgiving to intercession. This is a form of prayer that is very flexible; it obviously works better with a group that is at ease with each other and used to an informal style of prayer.

c Psalms are also great aids to group prayer because so many of them are prayers themselves. Once a group has spent some minutes in relaxation (just as important for the group as for the individual), it is useful to "pray" a psalm together. A reader will recite the psalm, leaving a long pause (a minute or more) after each verse. Each verse will trigger prayers from members of the group, who then share them aloud. The psalm supplies both the "triggering" ideas and also a structure, while leaving space for all manner of informal prayer.

These suggestions for use in small prayer group meetings are clearly not agendas for the whole meeting, but they might be useful aids when it comes time for specific prayer.

6   Retreats. By a retreat, I do *not* mean a conference. The object of a conference is to confer — we do all the talking. A conference is a time for a sharing of ideas and a planning of strategies and programs. In contrast, a retreat is a time to *listen* to God, and we should be geared to this single purpose.

What is the purpose of a retreat? It is a time (usually two to five days) when we go to a retreat centre in order to get away from all the busyness of our everyday lives. We do this, not in an attempt to escape from our day to day living, but in order to come back to it refreshed and renewed after having spent some time alone with God, time in which we have deliberately opened ourselves to him and listened to what he has to say to us. For many Christians, a regular time of retreat is a part of their ongoing spiritual life, and they try to plan a retreat once or twice a year. Some parishes organize a parish retreat (not to be confused with a "quiet day") every year, when a party of parishioners go away together, usually over a weekend. If this is not possible, there are often retreats organized by the diocese, or failing that, nearly all retreat houses will take in people who wish to make their own private retreats.

A retreat is usually either conducted or private. In a conducted retreat, the conductor (usually a priest, monk, or nun) gives a series of addresses designed to lead into a meditation. The day is also punctuated by regular meals and times of worship (matins, evensong, Eucharist, and compline); plenty of time is also allowed for private prayer, reading, and relaxation. A conductor is also available to give counselling and hear confessions if requested.

In a private retreat, there is no ordered program, other than times for meals and worship. The program is either left to the retreatant to decide, or it may be planned with the help of a priest. The only other variant to this that I have experienced is when a small group holds a retreat together and bases it upon a series of group meditations, which each one leads in turn.

One common feature of all retreats is *silence*. This is essential in order to relieve us from the need for conversation. Most of us are nervous of silence because our normal lives are saturated with a constant stream of noise. A welcome surprise to many on their first retreat is the discovery that silence can bring a special awareness of its own, and that in the silence of two or three days, God can speak to us powerfully. A retreat is an important ingredient in our prayer life. Room should be made for it and care taken to prepare for it properly, with the help of the parish priest.

7   A "Whole" Prayer Life. It is clear that there are many elements to a rich and full life of prayer. There are just as many ways of listening and talking with God as there are with our closest friends — indeed, there are more. The way to a "whole" life of prayer is to achieve a workable blend, combining all of these forms of prayer. Beginning with our determination to set aside time each day in order to pray, it is up to each of us to develop our own pattern. We shall include it in both vocal prayer and meditation, taking the trouble to read what others have written about their experiences, and being ready to share our experiences with others who, like us, are learning to know God better. If we are so drawn, we shall experience the gift of tongues and possibly be gifted with the ability to prophesy; these gifts will enhance our private prayer and will help us to minister in prayer for others. It is also important to share all this with at least one other person to whom we can be accountable; that person may, but need not, be our parish priest. Regardless, our confidant should be a person of prayer and experience. Whatever else, remember that if we want to live in Christ, prayer is the main element of his gift of life to us, and we will not get very far without it.

2

The Sacramental Life

Another set of God's lifelines to us is the sacraments, through which his life flows to us, renews us for day to day living, and strengthens us at special times in our lives. What do we mean by a sacrament?

We might well begin with a definition from the catechism of the Anglican Book of Common Prayer: "A sacrament is an outward and visible sign of an inward and spiritual grace."[5] This is not a profound theological statement, but it is a useful working definition. Perhaps we can begin by thinking of some examples of sacramental actions which are part of our daily lives. A handshake is a good one. When I meet my friend in the street, I feel a strong inward sense of pleasure. Yet merely to feel it inwardly is not enough; I want to express it in a way my friend will recognize, a way that will actually affect him. So I say: "Hello, John!" shake his hand, and slap him on the back. I could almost call this action sacramental in that it really does convey my sense of joy and happiness at seeing John again.

Now a sacrament (in the strictly religious sense) occurs when God shows his love and compassion to us through certain outward signs, such as the bread and the wine of Holy Communion. In a true sacrament, we go even deeper, for a sacrament is not simply a sign that shows how God loves us: it actually *conveys* the grace, the life, and the power of God. It is said that "a sacrament is a symbol (or sign) that actually conveys that which it symbolizes." Thus, the water of baptism not only *signifies* the new life which Christ promised to all who follow him; it actually *conveys* that new life. Again, in Holy Communion, the bread and wine do not just remind us of the Last Supper and all that Jesus said about being the "true bread that gives life to the world" (John 6.51); they actually bring the Last Supper into the present and convey the same "true bread," that life who is Christ himself. So a sacrament is a very powerful element in the

Christian's spiritual life, and it stands alongside prayer in any full life in Christ.

Thus, sacraments are specific gifts from God to help us to live fully in Christ. More particularly, they are gifts within the church. Just as the sap in the tree can only give its life to the branches and leaves that are part of it, so the grace we receive through the sacraments can only be received by those who are members of Christ's Body, the church. This is not to be exclusive, but simply to be precise; it is the reason why a non-Christian cannot receive Holy Communion.

This is what we mean by sacraments, but many questions still remain. How many sacraments are there? How do they function? What is their authority? What follows is a description of the sacraments of the church as they are commonly recognized within Catholic Christianity. (It will help in what follows to consult the diagram on page 42.)

The fifth Lateran Council in 1215 formally recognized seven sacraments as having been practised from the very earliest days of the church's existence. In making this statement, the church was not inventing anything new, but simply formalizing what had been the case almost from the beginning. Most of these sacraments could be traced right back to the Apostolic Church (as recorded in the New Testament); only in the case of marriage was there no such authority. Instead, the antiquity of marriage as a sacrament within the church was assumed to provide the necessary authority.

During the Reformation, the Protestant Churches in varying degrees rejected the sacraments as being unnecessary. The personal faith of each individual in his Saviour was held to be so all-important that little else (including sacraments) mattered. Some Protestant bodies (for example, the Quakers) rejected sacraments altogether. Others, like the Lutheran and Calvinist Churches, retained at least two — baptism and Holy Communion — and sometimes absolution as well. The Anglican Church, in a compromise, accepted the two "major sacraments" together with the others which were described as "commonly called sacraments." Today this distinction has become increasingly redundant, and all seven sacraments are practised in the Anglican Church.

How does a sacrament work? The scholars of the Middle Ages,

who were always anxious to define how things worked, said that there were four necessary elements in the effective practice of a sacrament. There had to be (a) a duly authorized minister, (b) the correct matter (bread, wine, water, etc.), (c) the proper form (the right words and actions), and (d) the intention. If we are tempted to think of this as unduly legalistic, the value of such an analysis becomes clear when we apply it to any of the sacraments. Taking the Eucharist as an example, a priest has to celebrate it, bread and wine must be available to consecrate, the words of our Lord at the Last Supper must be recalled, and the priest has to have the proper intentions for the service. When I am demonstrating Holy Communion to someone I am teaching, for example, it is not a true Eucharist because I am not intending it to be. (The diagram on page 42 has been divided into a number of columns in order to help us to understand further the working and the meaning of each of the sacraments.)

Holy Baptism

The intention of this sacrament is to initiate someone into the Christian faith, and so it marks the beginning of a person's life in Christ. Simply stated, this is how one becomes a Christian. Yet the moment we use the phrase "becoming a Christian," we should remember that a very great deal is tied up in these three words — nothing less, in fact, than the full meaning of the Christian drama! We shall be looking at the full meaning of baptism shortly, but first, some preliminary points. Who can administer baptism, and what is necessary for it to take place?

From the earliest days, it seems that the full act of initiation involved the bishop, who was the leader of the Christian community. He did not perform the whole ceremony, merely the latter part of the rite — the anointing and (somewhat later) the laying-on of hands. The washing or immersion in water was usually performed by a priest or even a layperson. And so, today, the pouring of water (what we have come to call baptism) may be performed by any baptized Christian, although it is normally done by a priest. Thus a hospital nurse who is herself baptized, has full authority to baptise a child who is in danger of dying. However, baptism is normally performed by the parish priest or his assistant in the presence of the local church community during the chief service on a Sunday morning.

Name	The Minister	The Matter and Form	The Intention	Authority
BAPTISM	Any baptised Christian but usually a priest.	Water, the words of baptism, and the signation.	Being reborn as a member of the church, entering into the new life, receiving the Holy Spirit.	Numerous. e.g. Matthew 28.18 Acts 8.38 Romans 6.5 Ephesians 4.5
CONFIRMATION	A bishop.	Laying-on of hands with prayer.	Receiving a strengthening gift of the Holy Spirit.	Acts 8.14–17
EUCHARIST	A priest	Bread, wine with the recital of the eucharistic prayer.	Receiving the "daily bread," Christ's renewing life for our own daily living.	Mark 14.22 ff. I Corinthians 11.17 ff.
ABSOLUTION	A priest	The words of absolution.	Restoration to God and the church after being separated by our sins.	John 20.22
HEALING	A priest (see text)	Laying-on of hands or anointing with oil.	Healing at physical, mental, and/or spiritual levels.	Acts 5.12 ff. 3.1 ff. James 5.13 ff.
MARRIAGE	A priest	The vows.	Receiving the grace or strength to build a marriage and family.	Later church traditions.
ORDINATION	A bishop	Laying-on of hands with prayers.	The setting apart of a deacon, priest, or bishop, and the receiving of the grace to fulfill that office.	Mark 3.13 and 6.6 Acts 6 I Timothy 4.14

The forms and materials of baptism are quite simple. All that is needed is water, coupled with words: "I baptise you, in the name of the Father, and of the Son, and of the Holy Spirit." In a clinical or emergency baptism, this is all that takes place. Following the pouring of water on the candidate's forehead comes the act of "signation," when the forehead is marked with the sign of the cross. Although this is often done with the water that has just been used for pouring, the signation has traditionally, and properly, been done with holy oil that has been blessed by the bishop. This latter practice has its roots in the anointing (or "Christening") with holy oil, which was seen as a symbol of the pouring out of God's Spirit on the anointed person. In baptism the act symbolizes the giving of the Holy Spirit to the new Christian, literally, the newly "anointed one."

What is the *intention* of these acts? Here we return again to the question of what it means to be a Christian. There are three requirements of a person seeking admission to the church, and these are summed up in the questions addressed to the candidate in the baptismal service. The candidate is asked:[6]

a To Renounce: to turn his back upon the world, the flesh, and the devil insofar as these are sinful and opposed to the will of God.

b To Believe: to state his faith in God, Father, Son, and Holy Spirit. This is usually done by reciting the Creed.

c To Commit: to commit his life to Jesus from now on.

The actual baptism then takes place. There are several elements, but it is possible to resolve them into two components.

1 The receiving of Jesus Christ as Saviour, with all this implies. To explain all the implications of this would itself fill a book, but they might be summarized by saying that Jesus is from now on placed at the centre of the person's life, breaking the stranglehold of sin. All that Saint Paul tries to explain in Romans (chapter 5) and Galatians (chapters 3 & 4) is now appropriated by the candidate. From now on Jesus is that person's Saviour, redeemer, reconciler, and victor over the power of sin. The candidate is now received into the Christian church which

Paul describes as Christ's Body; he is now a member, not of a kind of goodwill club, but of this mystical Body of Christ. To sum up, all that Christ lived and died for is now appropriated as the newly-baptized person becomes a "child of God and an inheritor of the kingdom."

All this is symbolized in the water of baptism. Not only is the water a symbol of cleansing from sin, it is also a symbol of rebirth. The candidate, by "drowning" to the old life and "emerging" to a totally new life is "born again." As one of the new baptism services puts it, "The old life is over; a new life is already begun."

2   The receiving of the Holy Spirit. Jesus did not tell us to start a new life in our own power. It is not enough simply to point a car in the right direction and hope it will move of its own accord. It needs gas to make it go. And Jesus knew that the same is true of us. We need more than just pointing in the right direction. This is why he promised that he would not leave us powerless but would send us the "Comforter" — literally, the strengthener. We shall be reading about this later and seeing how the promise was fulfilled historically at Pentecost and in the lives of the early Christians. In order for each of us to have power to live the new life (in fact, in order to *have* this new life) we each need our own personal Pentecost, and this is precisely what we receive in baptism. So, when a person is baptized, he not only receives Jesus as his personal Saviour and becomes a member of the Body of Christ; he also receives the gift of the Holy Spirit, the powerful life of that Body. And, in receiving the gift, he also receives all the gifts and blessings that the Holy Spirit has to shower upon him.

Holy baptism, then, marks the beginning of a person's life in Christ. In the promises, the candidate expresses repentance, faith, and commitment. In response, God's action is expressed through the symbols of water and the marking with the sign of the cross.

Confirmation

If baptism is the means by which we become Christians, receive the Holy Spirit, and are incorporated into the church, what is confirmation about? According to the tradition in which many of us were brought up, confirmation was regarded as the completion of our baptism, when we confirmed the vows that had been made for us when we were children. Confirmation was also the means by which we were admitted to the sacrament of Holy Communion. Yet this understanding of confirmation has been sharply questioned over the last few years and a new one is emerging.[7] Its outline is now clear.

Baptism, as I have just described it, is the sacrament of initiation, the means by which one becomes a Christian. A person is a ''full'' Christian from that moment onward. One has then received the Holy Spirit and, as a member of the Body of Christ, is able to share in the sacrament of Holy Communion. Confirmation is thus no longer regarded as the completion of a person's initiation, because it is not an integral part of becoming a Christian.

Then what is confirmation? The answer lies in the original meaning of the Latin word *confirmare* — to strengthen. It describes the way a person is strengthened or renewed by prayer and the laying-on of hands by the bishop. In the early church, this act of the bishop was part of the rite of initiation; the newly-made Christian (who had been immersed in water and anointed with oil) now received the laying-on of hands and a second anointing by the bishop, who prayed for the gift of the Holy Spirit. In the course of history, this episcopal act came to be separated from the baptism in water, sometimes by a gap of several years. Eventually, the laying-on of hands and the anointing by the bishop came to be regarded as a separate sacrament, related to but not part of the sacrament of baptism. As such, it passed into the Anglican tradition, where it underwent further transformation.

In the centuries that followed its original separation from baptism, confirmation came to be regarded as a means of strengthening (confirming). Although this aspect of the rite was overlaid with other meanings (especially in the Anglican tradition), such an interpretation is again being placed upon it today. We can therefore say that, in confirmation, a person comes before the bishop to receive a *strengthening* in the power of the Holy Spirit. It will take place when that person is ready to make an act of solemn affirmation and commitment to Jesus Christ, and can promise to take upon himself the vows that were originally made at his baptism. Clearly, this should not take place until a person is old enough to make such a decision, and we shall almost certainly see confirmation occur at a rather later age than it has in the recent past.

As a result of the power of confirmation, we believe that a real renewal takes place, and that all the gifts needed for a person's ministry in the church are poured out. Those who have witnessed a similar laying-on of hands at a charismatic service will no doubt notice a correspondence between the two events. There is, in fact, a close similarity: in each case the same Holy Spirit is at work, pouring out his grace upon the person being prayed for. In each case, we look for a renewal by the Spirit and the bestowal of spiritual gifts. Yet there is an important difference. In confirmation, the bishop is the minister; he is seen in his pastoral role, as "Father in God" to all those in his care. Moreover, his presence symbolizes that this is an act within the Holy Catholic Church, and that we are members, not just of a local congregation, but of the Holy Catholic Church of God, represented in the apostolic figure of the bishop.

Confirmation has, until recently, been regarded as something we had to go through before we could be admitted to Holy Communion. For many people, it will continue to be a traditional church act, usually occurring during one's early teenage years. Increasingly, however, children will receive Holy Communion without being confirmed; their confirmation will follow some years later, when they have decided that they really *do* believe the Christian faith and want to commit their lives to Christ. These two patterns will almost certainly coexist for many years. The basic meaning of the sacrament, however, is the same: confirmation is a means of strengthening and renewing our lives as Christians.

A Note About the Experience of Baptism in the Spirit in the Charismatic Movement

I have some hesitation about including this discussion in a chapter on the sacraments of the church, because it is not a sacrament. Yet there is so much confusion about the relationship of this experience to the traditional sacraments of baptism and confirmation that it would be wrong not to say something about it. What, then, is the nature of this "baptism in the Spirit?"

Clearly this is not a baptism in the sense in which the word is used either in the Bible or in the tradition of the church. It is a pity that this phrase came to be used, because it has caused a considerable amount of confusion for many people. It should properly be called a renewal in the Spirit.

We need to be clear that the Holy Spirit is undoubtedly given to us by our Lord when we are baptized, whether as infants or adults. Too often, however, we do not *appropriate* this gift to ourselves. It is as if we received the gift of a million dollars and immediately buried it in a hole, forgetting all about it. It is there all the time, but so hidden as to be useless. We do not know we have the money until we dig it up and spend it.

The experience of renewal in the Spirit seems to be something similar. We receive the new life of God in our baptism, usually as babies. But we have not deliberately appropriated it. At some later date, we need to do so. The charismatic movement has shown us how we can accomplish this, but it has also done something else. In demonstrating how God can come alive in us, the charismatic movement has also illustrated what Saint Paul meant when he used the words "gifts" and "fruits."

It now seems very clear that with the gift of the Holy Spirit come specific gifts, not for our own selfish use, but "for the building up of the Body (the local Christian community) in love" (Ephesians 4.12). Paul told us about these gifts — tongues, prophecy, discernment, teaching, pastoring, healing, etc. — and today we are beginning to relearn how every Christian is so gifted, not just the rector! This, in turn, is leading to a renewed understanding of ministry within the church. *All* are ministers; *all* have a job to do in the church, the goal of which is to bring about Christ's kingdom on earth. (We shall reflect on this again in the final chapter of part 1, on ministry.)

We are also relearning the meaning of the Pauline word "fruits"; the gift of the Spirit actually brings about a *transformation* of our lives. Many of us have grown up to hear the evangelistic message over the radio or television that Jesus will "change your life." It is now becoming abundantly clear that this does indeed happen, and that it is the action of the Holy Spirit living "within us." The reception and appropriation of the Holy Spirit should be expected to affect our lives completely with a new spirit of love, wholeness, and inner power. (To explore this experience more deeply, I would refer the reader to the many books on this subject which have been written during the last ten years. Several are listed in the bibliography.)

The Holy Eucharist

At the Last Supper, Jesus celebrated the first Eucharist with his apostles, and he commanded them to repeat this action afterwards. This command was obeyed by those apostles and then by their successors who came to be called bishops of the church (also called presbyters in some early documents). At first, it was only the bishops who presided at these Eucharists in the early church. Later, when the numbers of the congregations grew and it became impossible for the bishop to be present with all the local Christian communities on the Lord's Day, they ordained and authorized priests to take their place and be the "celebrants" at the liturgy. This has remained the primary function of the priest — to preside at the Eucharist. Within the Catholic (including Anglican) Churches, only the bishop or priest can perform this sacrament.

A word about names. It is ironic that the Eucharist, which should be the symbol of unity for all Christians, should have been such a focus of division in the past. Nowhere is this more evident than in the variety of names by which it is called and the strong emotions that have frequently been associated with those names. There are at least six names by which the sacrament is known, but the only difference is that each name tends to stress one particular aspect.

The Lord's Supper: This term emphasizes that it is essentially a meal around the Lord's table. Used most frequently by Protestant Churches.

Breaking of the Bread: A biblical phrase, used by the early church (Acts 2.42). It emphasizes the sense of fellowship engendered by breaking bread together. Not a common title; used chiefly by Protestant Churches.

The Mass: Derived from the final phrase of the old

Latin service, "Ite, missa est" (Go, you are sent out"). Emphasizes the idea that the sacrament equips us for service. Roman Catholic and Anglo-Catholic usage.

The Liturgy:

The word is of Greek origin, and means the "work of the people." It retains the idea of the sacrament as an act of the whole people. Chiefly used by Orthodox Christians.

Holy Communion:

The word means "fellowship" or "sharing." It emphasizes the role of the sacrament in binding the congregation together in their common life in Christ. Chiefly used by Anglicans; also used to denote that particular part of the service when the bread and wine are shared.

The Eucharist:

Simply the Greek term for "thanksgiving." The core of the service is the great central prayer of thanksgiving, and so this name came to be applied to the whole service. It was the most common name in the early church, and is the one most frequently used now, probably because it is acceptable to almost all Christians.

These are the names by which this sacrament is known. But what is the Eucharist? How did it begin? What happens in a celebration of the Eucharist, and as a sacrament, what does it convey? The best way to find the answers to these questions is to trace the development of the Eucharist from a biblical perspective. We can observe it developing in several stages.

1 During Jesus' Early Ministry. The daily supper which Jesus shared with his followers at the end of each day was a time of sharing, eating, drinking, and praying together. During these meals, Jesus' followers came to know and trust him as their leader and the source of their strength.

2 The Last Supper. This event took place during a traumatic evening in an upstairs room on the night of Jesus' arrest. He took bread and wine, identified them with his own body and blood, shared them with his followers, and commanded them to repeat what he had done ''in order to make me present'' (see 1 Corinthians 11.23).

3 Following His Crucifixion. It was a desolate, lonely time during which those same followers met for supper, acutely conscious that Jesus was no longer with them. It was a time of intense longing for his presence.

4 After His Resurrection. An amazing experience took place after the Resurrection: the risen Christ appeared with them at supper as they broke bread in a house at Emmaus (Luke 24.13 ff.), by a lakeside (John 21.2 ff.), and back in Jerusalem (Luke 24.33 ff.).

5 After Jesus' Ascension. Following Jesus' final disappearance (his Ascension), the disciples continued to obey his eucharistic command to ''do this'' and found that he was indeed with them in a mysterious presence. They associated this mystery with the bread and wine which they shared together.

6 Thereafter. This breaking of the bread was repeated whenever the disciples came together. As the church grew and subdivided into hundreds of Christian communities, each one continued to ''do this'' on the Lord's Day so that the risen Lord would be present with them. The practice has continued to this day.

Something of the awesome force of this tradition is conveyed in a well-known passage from a book of Dom Gregory Dix in which he describes what it has meant over many hundred years of the church's history.

> Was ever another command so obeyed? For century after century, spreading slowly to every continent and country and among every race on earth, this action has been done, in every conceivable human circumstance, for every conceivable human need from infancy and before it to extreme old age and after it, from the pinnacles of earthly greatness to the refuge of fugitives in the caves and dens of the earth. Men

have found no better thing than this to do for kings at their crowning and for criminals going to the scaffold; for armies in triumph or for a bride and bridegroom in a little country church; for the proclamation of a dogma or for a good crop of wheat; for the wisdom of the Parliament of a mighty nation or for a sick old woman afraid to die; for a schoolboy sitting an examination or for Columbus setting out to discover America; for the famine of whole provinces or for the soul of a dead lover; in thankfulness because my father did not die of pneumonia; for a village headman much tempted to return to fetich because the yams had failed; because the Turk was at the gates of Vienna; for the repentance of Margaret; for the settlement of a strike; for a son for a barren woman; for Captain so-and-so, wounded and prisoner of war; while the lions roared in the nearby amphitheatre; on the beach at Dunkirk; while the hiss of scythes in the thick June grass came faintly through the windows of the church; tremulously, by an old monk on the fiftieth anniversary of his vows; furtively, by an exiled bishop who had hewn timber all day in a prison camp near Murmansk; gorgeously, for the canonisation of S. Joan of Arc — one could fill many pages with the reasons why men have done this, and not tell a hundredth part of them. And best of all, week by week and month by month, on a hundred thousand successive Sundays, faithfully, unfailingly, across all the parishes of christendom, the pastors have done this just to *make* the *plebs sancta* Dei — the holy common people of God.[8]

The Eucharist is thus a means by which our Lord becomes present to the Christian community gathered in his name. As such, it is the central act of the church, the occasion when it comes together week by week, to meet its Lord and to be renewed by him as the Last Supper is re-enacted. Corporately, it is the renewal and the recreation of the local church each week; individually, it is the daily bread upon which we feed for spiritual strength. When we come to Holy Communion, we come to meet our Lord. We meet him in the bread and wine which we consume; we meet him in the loving presence of those who are gathered with us; we meet him who is the host at the table; we meet him who has laid down his life so that he might share it with us. We remember his life, death, resurrection, and ascension, not simply as past history but as present realities, as we reflect on how he died and rose again for us and for our world.

The material and forms of the Eucharist are the staple diet of daily life — bread and wine, with the words and actions of our Lord at the Last Supper. There are many ways in which this has been said and done, from the mystery and complexity of a three hour Orthodox liturgy (sung to traditional Byzantine chants), to a simple ceremony said around a living-room table. Each part of the church has evolved its own ways of celebrating the Eucharist. For four hundred years the Anglican Church has used a form substantially written by Archbishop Cranmer in 1549 and found in the Book of Common Prayer. Today, however, we are living in an age of reform. Most churches within the Anglican Communion have composed contemporary forms of the liturgy, which are often used side by side with that from the Prayer Book.

Absolution

If baptism is the means by which we become Christians, and the Eucharist serves to renew us week by week, then absolution is the sacrament by which we are restored to God when our relationship has been broken by sin.

The sacrament of absolution is also popularly called confession or penance, but strictly speaking, these words refer simply to two of the things we do when we come for absolution. We also use the word *confession* in a number of other settings — which, of course, adds to the confusion — so it might be helpful to define the term at this point.

Confession is the simple (but by no means easy) recital of our sins to God, which should be a part of our everyday vocal prayers. We should regularly and privately reflect upon where we have gone wrong during the day (or since we last confessed), and simply tell God about it, asking him to forgive us.

When the whole congregation comes before God on Sunday morning, it seems right that, as a community, it should confess its sins and shortcomings before proceeding with the rest of the worship. At matins, evensong, and even more important, in the Eucharist, we find prayers of corporate confession. These are not primarily meant for us as individuals; we should have offered such prayers before coming to church. Corporate confession is meant for us as the people of God, getting things straight with God before going on with our worship.

Both of these forms of confession are necessary, but they are not to be confused with the *sacrament* of absolution, in which we make a personal confession to God in the presence of a priest. There seem to be at least three reasons why this sacramental form of confession and absolution is valuable. First of all, it is difficult, demanding a degree of humility and concreteness that is all too easy to avoid if we are just saying a confession by ourselves. Second, it takes place before another Christian. Not only does this demand an act of loving trust, but it reminds us that, when we sin, we do so not only against God but against our fellow Christians — one rotten apple affects the whole barrel. The fact that our confession of sin is shared with another Christian means that healing takes place, not only between the penitent and God, but between fellow Christians in the church. Third, it is valuable simply because Jesus gave us this means of receiving his forgiveness and love, for he gave his apostles the charge: "If you forgive the sins of any, they are forgiven; if you retain the sins of any, they are retained" (John 20.23). This authority is specifically given to every priest at his ordination. It seems to me that, if we are offered a gift like this, we should take it with joy.

"But confession is Roman Catholic!" Yes, of course it is — so is Bible reading, prayer, communion, almsgiving, and all the other things that Christians should do! There seems to be no reason why Anglicans (or other Christians whose churches retain this sacrament) should spurn something just because they feel that others may have abused it in the past! In fact, the Anglican Church has never rejected it. Anglicans are positively encouraged to use this sacrament in the Book of Common Prayer (see pages 91 and 581). Traditionally Anglicanism has taught that: "None must; all may; some should" use sacramental confession.

If we feel this sacrament is something we might consider using, either to deal with a particularly onerous sin or as part of our ongoing spiritual discipline, it would be useful to read

How to Make Your Confession by Butterfield.[9] This short booklet will explain how to go about preparing a confession, and what to do when we go to make it in front of a priest. Better still, it is advisable to raise the subject with either our parish priest or another who regularly hears confessions, and to ask his or her guidance.

One further word: it is an absolute rule that nothing said or heard in a confession may afterwards be repeated by the priest, *even with the person who made the confession*, unless of course it is later brought up by the person making it. It is as if the words had never been uttered. I think many people are scared of going to a priest for confession because, ''I could never look him in the face again!'' On the contrary, even though my mind goes blank immediately after having heard a confession, I always (as a priest) feel a tremendous sense of compassion and closeness to a penitent, so that it constitutes one of the most humbling and joyous aspects of my ministry.

The essential image behind the sacrament of absolution is that of Jesus facing the repentant sinner and saying: ''Your sins are forgiven; go and sin no more'' (John 8.11). These words are as direct today as they were some two thousand years ago, through the sacrament available to all those who choose to receive it.

Healing

For centuries, this sacrament was called ''unction'' or even ''extreme unction.'' Until quite recently it was seen as a form of anointing a person in preparation for death. Yet in the early days of the church's life, unction began as an act of healing; when you received it, you hoped and expected to get better! The reason for this change in the practice of the sacrament is intimately bound up with the gradual decline of the healing ministry in the church in the Middle Ages.[10] Following the revival of that ministry in our own time, the sacrament of healing is again being restored to its proper place.

The truth is that spiritual healing (or healing through prayer) was at the very centre of our Lord's ministry. It was as a healer that he attracted such crowds; and he was obviously highly successful, or else crowds would not have come to see and touch him in such great numbers. Historically, we have always accepted the fact that Jesus in his own time forgave sins, and the church has always insisted that this is one of its prime functions. Yet, although a great deal is told about Jesus in the Gospels as a healer, we have almost totally ignored this healing ministry in our own day. Thankfully, this error is being corrected, and we are now seeing a rediscovery of an effective ministry of healing in the church. (Much has been and is being written about this, and I draw attention to several useful books in the bibliography.)

It would help if we were somewhat clearer about what is meant by a ministry of healing, and particularly the sacrament of healing. Here are some basic definitions:

Faith Healing. This is *not* what we are talking about within the church. Faith healing, as the name implies, is achieved through the faith of the person involved: it may take place regardless of their belief or unbelief in God. It has to do with the school of thought that says, ''I can do anything if I set my mind to it.'' Psychosomatic medicine is teaching us that there is indeed a definite link between the state of our mind and the health of our body, so that faith healing can undoubtedly work in some cases. The fatal weakness of such a means of healing, however, is that it obviously depends upon a person's faith; sadly, this is so often one of the things most lacking in a sufferer.

Spiritual or Prayer Healing. Here we are on firmer ground; there is a genuine revival of this gift within the church. Spiritual healing is based upon the simple truth that the Lord who created our bodies is also able to renew and heal them, and he will do so if we ask him in prayer. How he does this is a mystery, but the evidence that he does heal people is overwhelming. Sometimes it is clear that certain people are specially gifted by the Holy Spirit with a particular ability to heal. This seems to happen far more frequently than we would suppose, although we should not be surprised about such gifts if we have been reading the Acts of the Apostles with an open mind. Such an ability will be discovered among those who are openly seeking the gift of the Holy Spirit in a congregation, and it undoubtedly grows as it is nourished and practised.

Quite apart from such gifts bestowed on individuals, God

undoubtedly answers prayers for healing both from individuals and particularly from groups of Christians who pray together. Sometimes such healing takes place instantly, but more often, prayer is answered gradually as the group or individual continues to pray (often with the laying-on of hands) over an extended period. Many parishes now have groups meeting regularly to pray together for the sick. They also often have networks of people who, on receipt of a phone call, will stop and pray for those in urgent need.

The Sacrament of Healing. The actual sacrament of healing is a part of the ordained ministry of the priest, who acts as mediator of the grace of Christ for a sick person. It may be performed solemnly within a service of healing and in the presence of others; but perhaps more frequently it will be part of the priest's ongoing ministry, when he or she is visiting the sick in hospital or at home.

It is performed in either (or both) of two ways. In accordance with the injunctions of the Epistle of St James (chapter 5.13), the sick person is anointed with oil, together with the recitation of prayers for his recovery. Remember that oil (or ointment) was commonly used as the means of treating wounds in the ancient world, so that its symbolic use in spiritual healing is quite natural. We have an example of the traditional medication being blessed so that it might perform not only its normal healing function, but also be used by God as a means of special divine healing. (Of course I am not suggesting here that God does not equally use quite normal methods of healing, such as those performed through the treatment of the medical profession.) In addition to the actual anointing, and frequently instead of it, the priest will simply lay hands on the sick person and pray for healing. An order for the sacramental ministry to the sick will be found in the Book of Common Prayer. Because this healing ministry has so long been neglected or misunderstood within the life of the church, it will be valuable to read some of the excellent books that have been written on the subject. Particularly useful are those by Agnes Sandford and Father Francis MacNutt, which are noted in the bibliography.

Marriage

Marriage is the late comer as a sacrament of the church. We do not find any direct authority or precedent for it in the New Testament. Marriage in the Roman Empire was (as it also is now) a civil contract made by husband and wife, and recognized as binding in law. When Christians were married, the ceremony was recognized under Roman civil law, but as Christians they quite naturally sought the blessing of God upon their new vocation as a married couple. This blessing came to have the significance of a sacrament, especially when the church began to be recognized by the state as having the legal authority to solemnize marriages.

In our own day a couple can, of course, be married by a civil registrar, and the church fully recognizes the marriage. There is no suggestion that a couple who has not been married in church are "living in sin!" When a couple chooses to be married by a priest, however, a new *sacramental* dimension is added, and their marriage is graced by the Holy Spirit. This is based very simply upon the idea that, in any new venture in life, God will give us a special blessing of his Holy Spirit to strengthen us. All we have to do is to ask and be open to him. So, in marriage, husband and wife come to ask God for his blessing; then, through the mediation of the priest, the prayer is answered. Legally, there is no distinction between a civil and a church wedding. The vital difference is that in the former the couple are on their own, whereas in the latter case, they have invited and received the Holy Spirit into their newly joined lives as a continuing presence for the building up of their marriage.

Ordination

We shall see later on in chapter 9 how the ministry of the church developed in the very early days of its life. In the beginning, Christ chose and trained a team of twelve apostles, and finally commissioned them to go out as leaders of the new movement. In the Book of Acts, we read of them going out and adding others (Matthias and Paul) to their number as the demands of the growing church increased. We see the church continuing to expand, and other apostolic men such as Timothy and Titus being appointed as leaders of the new communities spreading all over the Roman Empire. These leaders were given the name "episcopoi" (superintendents or bishops), and they were charged with the total responsibility of all those in their care. It was their special function to preside at the regular Eucharist, to restore the penitent sinner, to see that the Gospel was proclaimed, to teach and guard the faith, and to protect the unity of the catholic ("universal" or "orthodox") church. Very soon after the New Testament was written, we find the names of others, like Ignatius of Asia Minor and Clement of Rome, who were leaders of such communities.

At one point, still within the period of the New Testament (Acts 6), we read that the total care of these growing communities became too much; bishops were having to spend a disproportionate amount of their time in day to day administration. So seven deacons were chosen and set apart to look after these affairs, in order to free the leaders for their episcopal tasks. These deacons (the name means "servant") continued in this role and also came to be assistants at the Eucharist, taking the consecrated bread to the sick after the liturgy on Sundays. And so the two "orders" of bishop and then deacon evolved in the early church.

As the church expanded still further, the order of priests came into being — persons who had received the delegated authority from their bishop for the oversight of the smaller Christian communities. It was their particular task to preside at the Eucharist and to forgive sins, as well as to carry out the more general duties of pastoral care and government.

In this way the three orders of ministry in the church came into being: the bishop with the full apostolic authority of Christ himself, and the priests and deacons having delegated functions within the church. The sacrament of ordination is best described in the words of the Prayer Book as a form "for the making of Bishops, Priests and Deacons."[11] The only person who is authorized to perform an ordination is the bishop, because only in him does the full apostolic authority lie. When a new bishop is consecrated, at least three other bishops take part, in order to express the corporate nature of the act and to represent the authority of the Holy Catholic Church. At the ordination of a priest, the bishop usually invites several other priests to share with him in the laying-on of hands, to emphasize that it is a shared ministry into which the new priest is being ordained. The form of the sacrament — for bishop, priest, or deacon — is always this laying-on of hands by the bishop(s), together with the prayer commissioning the ordinand to his or her new ministry. As a result of the sacrament, the new priest, bishop, or deacon receives both the authority for a new role in the church and also the grace to do it.

What do bishops, priests, and deacons actually do? Most of us have only a very hazy idea about this, our experience having usually been confined to the ministry of our local rector and the occasional visit of the diocesan bishop. In practice, however, they actually perform a great variety of functions within the church, and are described by a rich variety of names. In order to help us clarify this, it might be useful to think of bishops, priests, and deacons as three commissioned "ranks" of clergy. The many other titles by which they are called can be thought of as functions which they perform in the church's total ministry.

1 Bishops:

Diocesan Bishop. The most common position held by a bishop is that of pastor of a diocese. In Anglican (and Orthodox) understanding, diocesan bishops all have equal authority within the total ministry of the church.

Archbishop. For the purposes of administration, an archbishop is the senior bishop of an ecclesiastical Province (or group of dioceses). There are four such Provinces in Canada. As senior bishop of a province, an archbishop is sometimes called a metropolitan. The senior bishop in a *country* is referred to as the Primate, and as such, is the chairman of the House of Bishops and spokesman for the national church.

A Suffragan or Assistant Bishop, as the names imply, is a bishop who has no diocesan jurisidiction but is assistant to a diocesan.

Note: In the Roman Catholic Church, certain senior bishops who are members of the electoral college (to elect a Pope) are called cardinals. The Pope, besides being Bishop of Rome, is also regarded by Roman Catholics as being Christ's "vicar" on earth, and all other bishops are subject to him. This concept is not shared by the Anglican or Orthodox Churches, and this constitutes the major difference separating them from Rome.

2   Priests:

Rector or Vicar. The distinction between the names stems from the time when vicars were appointed and paid by a corporate body, whereas rectors lived off the "greater tithe" paid by the parishioners. The rector is also the *curate* (having the "cure" or care of souls within the parish), but this title is today given more frequently to an assistant.

Dean. A priest with oversight of a cathedral, a dean is usually second in seniority to the bishop in a diocese.

Rural/Urban Dean. For administrative reasons, parishes were traditionally grouped into deaneries of anything between a half to two dozen parishes. The rural dean is the senior priest or the chairman among the clergy of the deanery.

Archdeacon. At another level of administration, between the deanery and the diocese, is the archdeaconry. The archdeacon is the bishop's administrative officer within this archdeaconry, and usually works closely with the bishop in the administration of the diocese. Quite often, an archdeacon does not have such a geographical base, and is simply an administrative assistant to the bishop.

Canon. Originally, canon was the title given to a priest who was living under a "canonical rule" and usually attached to a cathedral. Now the title of canon is commonly given (a) as a courtesy title to priests who have served the church faithfully for many years or in some special way, or (b) to a priest who holds some administrative function in a diocese.

Chaplain. Many priests are not attached to parishes but have special pastoral responsibilities as chaplains in institutions such as schools, hospitals, colleges, prisons, the armed forces, or in industry.

3   Deacons:

As we have seen, deacons were originally appointed as administrators to relieve the bishop to do his episcopal duties. In time, however, the diaconate has become virtually a probationary period before becoming a priest. As such, a deacon is usually an assistant *curate* in a parish. There is a move currently to establish a more permanent diaconate to be co-workers with a parish priest.

3

Worship

The chief resource book for the Christian is the Bible but, for
the Anglican, there has for over four hundred years been the various Books of Common Prayer, usually called the Prayer Book.
They have provided the Anglican not only with a book for worship but also a standard for faith and doctrine. They have served
the church well during this period but, over the last fifty years,
a worldwide movement for liturgical change has resulted in the
development of new Prayer Books in most parts of the Anglican Communion. In Canada, this has led to the production of
The Book of Alternative Services, which is steadily taking the
place of the old Prayer Book in our worship. We shall therefore
look at this new book as well as the old, tracing their origins
and becoming familiar with their contents.

Origins. One of the marks of catholicity in the Anglican Church
is that it does indeed have a Prayer Book. At the time of the
Reformation (see Chapter 9), such formal worship was often
questioned by many of the new Protestant Churches. For example, the minister was sometimes given an outline of what he
must say and do rather than verbatim text. The Anglican
reformers chose not to take this course but rather to retain the
ordered, liturgical worship of the Catholic Church. However,
it was not preserved without substantial change. With this in
mind, Thomas Cranmer, the Archbishop of Canterbury, set
about composing a completely new Prayer Book. It was to be
in English and used not only by the clergy but also by everyone. To do this, Cranmer drew from the existing liturgical books
of the Catholic Church and, like the other reformers, sought
to give the new book a substantially more biblical flavour. The
core of his new book were the services of Holy Communion,

Morning and Evening Prayer, to which were added orders of service for other special occasions.

The first edition of Cranmer's new Prayer Book was published in 1549, at a time when the English Church was about to enter a very Protestant phase. It was soon criticised for not being Protestant enough and a new edition with a more reformist flavour was published in 1552. This text remained in use with minor changes for over one hundred years until 1662, when the Church of England, having experienced a bitter civil war and a decade of puritan government, set itself on a more Catholic course. It began by revising its Prayer Book along more Catholic lines. This, by and large, is the Prayer Book which has come down to us. In Canada, a revision was made in 1918 in order to adapt it to Canadian use. Finally, in 1962, another revised edition was published in an attempt to update it and bring it more into line with current liturgical ideas. It remains the official book of the Anglican Church of Canada. Let us consider it under three headings.

A   The Daily Prayers of the Church

Until the time of Archbishop Cranmer, there had been no formal prayers of this kind for ordinary people to use. However, the monks, nuns and clergy had always had an obligation to recite the Divine Offices daily. Altogether, eight services were to be said (either together "in choir" or alone) every day. These offices are still sung in many religious houses and are known as matins, lauds, prime, terce, sext, none, vespers, and compline. When Cranmer came to compose his new Prayer Book, he intended these services to be translated and simplified so that everyone could say them. So he translated them into English and abbreviated them into two daily offices which we call matins (or morning prayer) and evensong. Every priest was exhorted to say them daily in his church (and to summon the people to join him by ringing the church bell!) and all were invited to use them whether in church or at home. Cranmer's ideal vision was at least partially realized. Since his time the new daily offices have been faithfully said by clergy and lay readers, day by day. To a lesser degree, they have been used by the general laity, although never to the extent envisioned by the archbishop. However, the idea of daily Bible reading, reflection, and prayer has

remained at the heart of Anglican spirituality. As a full congrega-
tional service, matins is today found in fewer and fewer churches
on a Sunday morning. Similarly, evensong is rarely sung as a
corporate service except in a few city parishes, often where there
is a good choir to attract a faithful following.

The Holy Communion or Eucharist has increasingly become
the focus of Anglican corporate worship, especially on Sunday
mornings. The tradition of the Apostolic Church was to "break
bread" on the Lord's Day. Right from the start, the Sunday
Eucharist has been the regular weekly service of the Christian
Church. The actual service of Holy Communion in the 1962
Prayer Book was composed by Archbishop Cranmer largely
using the existing Latin Mass as his model, but carefully adapt-
ing it to avoid what he considered to have been its "supersti-
tious errors."

Both the Daily Offices and the service of Holy Communion
demanded that there be organised readings, psalms, and prayers
to be used for every day of the year. This need, in fact, went
right back to the early church, when the early Christians realized the need for an organised way of reading the scriptures and
saying the psalms. And so, very early on, and especially in
monastic settings, the day by day "propers" of the church year
came into being. These contained the readings, psalms and
proper prayers and they were organised according to two prin-
ciples. First of all, in the monastic night office (and to a lesser
extent in public worship) there was the desire to spread the reading of scriptures and the reciting of psalms over the year, so as
to ensure that as much as possible of the Bible was covered and
the psalms said over a weekly (later monthly) cycle. So readings were appointed for each day of the year, together with
appropriate psalms and prayers.

The second principle was that these propers should also reflect
the church's calendar. This calendar as it eventually developed
was based partly on the great seasons of the church year (such
as Christmas, Easter, and Pentecost) but also on the increasing
number of Saints' Days. These latter grew in number until by
Cranmer's time, the whole year was almost filled with them.

In the new Prayer Book, Cranmer abbreviated the number of
the old propers and greatly simplified the calendar of saints. The
result was the calendar (on page ix) together with two sets of
propers, one based on the Sundays of the year and the greater

festivals (Christmas, Ash Wednesday, etc.) and another comprising readings and prayers for a much reduced list of saints. These propers lasted right through to the Canadian book of 1962.

Within this section on the Daily Prayers should also be included the Litany, a petitionary prayer to be used responsively with the congregation and intended to be used especially at certain times of the church year.

B   The Sacraments of the Church

These comprise the next category of services in the Prayer Book, although the arrangement is not quite so tidy as one might desire! The sacraments (other than the Eucharist) are included.

1   Holy Baptism (page 522) appears in two forms. One is for the baptism of infants, while the other is for adults or, as the Prayer Book puts it, "those of riper years." The difference is simply that in the latter the candidate is able to answer for himself rather than having the godparents speak on his behalf. This service was designed to be used outside the usual Sunday liturgy and does not fit easily into the present-day practice of baptism within the context of the main Sunday Eucharist.

2   The Catechism (page 544) or "an instruction to be learned . . . before confirmation" is an attempt by the Anglican Church formally to make a clear statement of what a Christian is expected to believe. Nowadays it is rarely learned by rote as it used to be, but is a useful summary of many things that this present book is trying to explain. It is immediately followed by the sacrament of *Confirmation* (page 556).

3   The Solemnization of Matrimony (page 563) is designed to be used either with or without communion although not easy to use with the latter. If it is followed by communion, then special propers follow.

4   The Ordering of Deacons and Priests and the Consecration of Bishops (page 637). It is somewhat confusing to find this sacrament separated from the others by some seventy pages. However, it was probably not part of the original 1549 *BCP*, but published a year later, and then annexed to subsequent Prayer Books.

5, 6 The Sacraments of Healing and Reconciliation are some-what hidden in the Prayer Book but they do in fact appear in a section called the *Ministry to the Sick* (page 576). It is unfortunate that the second of these has been associated only with the sick, which would seem to suggest both that sickness is a result of sin and also that absolution is important only when a person is gravely ill. In practice, however, the section dealing with reconciliation may be used quite independently from the rest. As we saw before, the sacrament of healing may be used either with the laying on of hands or by anointing with oil.

C A Supplement of Additional Material

The rest of the 1962 Prayer Book is made up of a variety of material which I do not need to explain in detail, although it still merits attention. There are other occasional offices and services for special occasions. Most frequently used (by the clergy at least) is the burial office. Others are referred to less often. The Penitential Office has traditionally been said on Ash Wednesday, the Harvest Thanksgiving only at the time of harvest. There is a form of service for the consecration of a new church and one for the induction of a new rector to a parish. We are told how to bless a foundation stone (page 677) or a new churchyard (page 692). There are prayers for sailors at sea (page 628), (although none for airmen in flight), prayers of thanksgiving for a new baby (page 573), prayers for young people (page 622), and prayers to be said by a family (page 722). Finally, there are two statements of faith, one of which is an ancient creed of the whole church (page 695) and the other a statement of the theological position of the Church of England at the time of Queen Elizabeth I (page 698). During a dull sermon, there is more than enough at the back of the Prayer Book to keep us interested!

This, then, is the traditional Book of Common Prayer. In its essential form it has, for over four hundred years, been common to all Anglicans throughout the world, expressing a unity of faith and practice and has served as a means of binding together the many branches of the Anglican Communion. However, the last thirty or so years have seen the development of new prayer books throughout the Anglican Communion and it is to one of these that we now turn.

Toward a New Prayer Book

Although not radical, the 1962 Canadian Prayer Book made possible the climate for change and, as a result, there has been pressure to produce a completely new book almost since its publication. Why this need for change? The simple answer is that the times have changed dramatically since the days of Archbishop Cranmer. Our world is radically different from the one which people explored in the sixteenth century. It is no longer a world of kings and queens and we no longer cross the ocean in small wooden sailing ships. Science and technology have altered not only our thinking but also our ability to control or destroy our environment. The French and Marxist revolutions have produced a totally new attitude towards society and government. Psychology and sociology have blown apart our former ideas of humankind and how we behave in society. And, although many people in today's world believe in the God of the Bible, many do not and the variety of religious beliefs is legion.

We also need to remember that any prayer book must necessarily speak to and express the needs of people at a particular point in history. To that extent, it is bound to mirror that period with all its assumptions and attitudes, not to mention its biases and prejudices. So the question has arisen as to whether a book that was written for the subjects of the first Elizabeth can meet the needs of those living in a very different world four hundred years later, a world, for example, in which women are no longer to be excluded by language or "given away" at their wedding.

And there are other changes as well. Our understanding of worship itself has changed significantly since the Book of Common Prayer was written. Scholars now know far more about the origins and history of Christian worship and so we are able to compare what seem to be the leadings of the Holy Spirit with our more recently acquired knowledge of past tradition. The ecumenical movement has also had a marked effect upon liturgical thought. As the different churches have drawn closer, they have increasingly worked together and the results of this are evident in the new liturgies they have produced. Again, religious insights have changed over four hundred years. Today, we are much more deeply aware of the church as the body of Christ, an organic body set within the world. Baptism has been restored to its critically important place as a sign of the beginning of a person's new life in this new community. The Eucharist has been restored to its place as the central act of the Christian community on the Lord's Day. The importance of both word and sacrament are now central in equipping the people of God for their active service in the world. And it is the task of liturgy to express these insights in the ways we worship together. The need for a new Prayer Book has been clear for a long time. Out of all this has come the new Canadian *Book of Alternative Services*.

The actual envisioning and planning for the new book began not too long after the ink on the 1962 book had dried! On the authority of General Synod, the Doctrine and Worship Committee of the church began to publish a series of booklists with experimental forms of service for a wide variety of occasions such as marriage, burial, communion, baptism, etc. These were all duly tested and revised in the light of experience until, in 1985, General Synod gave its approval to the new *Book of Alternative Services*.

The Book of Alternative Services

Just what is in this new book? How are we to find our way about it? Fortunately, this is made easy for us by eight very helpful divisions which are clearly laid out in the contents.

1 The Divine Office

As in the old Prayer Book, the offices of Morning and Evening Prayer consist of a pattern of psalms, readings from scripture, canticles (literally "songs"), and prayers, a form of service which had its roots in the synagogue worship of the Jews. They are preceded by a penitential rite (page 45) to be used at the discretion of the minister or parish worship committee. The special readings, psalms and prayers appointed for each day are to be found in the Proper of the Church Year. A particular hallmark of this section of the *B.A.S.* might be noted at this point. Unlike the Prayer Books, it is designed to be much more flexible in its use, allowing for a greater variety. This puts a greater demand on both those who are leading and planning the services and those taking part. At its worst, this can result in confusion but, with care and imagination, it can result in a greatly enriched experience of worship.

2   Baptism and Reconciliation

In the the *B.A.S.*, baptism has thankfully been lifted out of the obscurity it has long suffered and been given the high profile it should command. It marks, after all, the most fundamental Christian experience of which all else is an extension, i.e., the act of becoming a Christian and entering into the new life in Christ. As the rubrics (directions) on page 150 make clear, it is to be celebrated in the presence of the whole Christian community at the chief Sunday Eucharists and the service itself is shaped with this in mind. It differs radically from the form of baptism in the *Book of Common Prayer* in two important respects. It is designed not as a private family service but as a rite to be performed in the context of the parish community and involving all present in renewing their own baptismal covenant. Secondly, the rather narrow focus of the old rite on salvation from sin is replaced with a much more balanced understanding of baptism as the incorporation into the body of Christ, the receiving of the Holy Spirit and an emphasis upon what it means to live the Christian life out in the world at large. By making provision for the rite of confirmation in the service, the new rite also recognises that baptism and confirmation really belong together in the one, single act of initiation as a Christian.

Immediately after baptism are two orders for the *Reconciliation of a Penitent*, the second a shorter form than the first. They belong here for the simple reason that it is the baptismal relationship that is being continually broken by sin and needs to be restored by an act of reconciliation. The inclusion of these two orders fills a considerable gap in the old Prayer Book and their welcome is to be seen in their increasing use in the church today.

3   The Holy Eucharist

The form of the Eucharist in the *B.A.S.* has been much influenced both by the studies of the older liturgies of the early church and by liturgical developments in the contemporary churches. The order of service beginning on page 185 allows for considerable flexibility, includes six possible forms of Eucharistic Prayer (page 193 to 210), and is very similar to the contemporary liturgies of other churches. Because of the high regard with which the old Prayer Book service of Holy Communion is still held, that material is also included but in the pattern and structure of the contemporary rite, beginning on page 230.

4 The Proper of the Church Year

Right at the front of the *B.A.S.* we have a calendar of saints. Then, beginning on page 261, we find a section called the Proper of the Church Year. This contains two broad sections. The first includes prayers, psalms, and readings for all the Sundays of the year and is based on the annual cycle of the church's seasons. Thus it begins at Advent and continues through Christmas, etc., until the very last Sunday called The Reign of Christ. A welcome inclusion to this section are special liturgies for such important times as Ash Wednesday, Holy Week, and Easter. Then, still within this section, (page 398 ff), there are special propers appointed for the saints' days and holy days, according to the calendar at the beginning of the book.

The second broad section, called the Lectionary, consists of the readings and psalms appointed for every day of the year. These again are organised in two tables. The first (page 452) contains the readings to be used for the daily offices while the second is a similar list to be used for weekday Eucharists throughout the year. In this way, every day has its appointed readings, the greater proportion of the Bible is read through every three years and the psalter is recited several times a year. We will find these lectionaries very useful as a way of organising our own personal Bible reading in a balanced way and a number of programmes are published to help follow the Bible in this way.

5 Pastoral Offices

These services might well be described as a series of "rites of passage" to mark four particular stages in our lives, i.e., our birth, marriage, sickness, and death. There are two orders for *Marriage*, one with and one without Holy Communion. We might note the emphasis today upon rites such as these being celebrated within the context of the Eucharist, baptism, confirmation, and funerals being other examples.

The revived interest in healing has resulted in the old order for the *Visitation of the Sick* having a much higher profile in the new *Ministry to the Sick*, with provision made for the laying-on of hands and the anointing with oil.

There are no less than three different orders for a *Funeral*, together with a new form of ministry which can be performed at the time of death. These together provide a flexibility which is welcome in light of the the changing social patterns to do with funerals. Again, there is the implied expectation that funerals for those who have been communicants in their lives should take place within the context of the Eucharist.

Finally, the Pastoral Offices include a service of *Thanksgiving for the Gift of a Child*. This is not meant to be in any sense a substitute for baptism. It is simply what it says, a chance to thank God for the gift of a child. It comes as a response to both the natural desire of parents who want to thank God for their new baby and also an opportunity for clergy to respond positively to parents when an immediate baptism is considered inappropriate. It may precede baptism or may equally be used when parents and clergy have decided to postpone baptism until later. It replaces a rite whose title included the words "the Churching of Women."

6   Episcopal Offices

As the title implies, these offices are to be administered by the bishop alone. They include an order for *Confirmation*, when it is not being celebrated within the context of a baptism service. There are also orders for the sacraments of *Ordination* to each of the three ordained ministries of the church, i.e., the diaconate, the priesthood, and the episcopate. In addition to these, there is also a rite for *The Blessing of Oil* to be used in baptism (called the "chrism") and the anointing of the sick. This rite is normally to be used in the cathedral as part of the Maundy Thursday ceremonies.

7   Parish Thanksgivings and Prayers

With the increasing importance being attached to family prayers today, it is helpful to have a very practical framework of prayers for the home or for small informal groups. This section also includes a form of prayer to be used for the anniversary of a dedication. There are, as well, two useful collections of prayers on a wide variety of topics, one for use in church, the other to be used in the home.

8   The Psalter

The Psalter is a translation from the Hebrew of the Book of Psalms in the Old Testament. The psalms are simply the hymns of the Jewish people which were taken over and have been used by Christians right from the beginning. Many translations have been made, especially this last fifty years. That in the *B.A.S.* is the same as the translation in the Episcopal Church's *Prayer Book* and was selected both because of its familiar form and also its suitability for singing to plainchant and Anglican chant.

The psalms express a great wealth of human sentiment and come from a variety of backgrounds. Some are intensely personal, expressing personal emotions of sorrow and frustration, joy and hope. Others are public and civic, originally composed for such events as a royal wedding (Ps.45), a national festival, or a victory. Today, they form an integral part of the daily offices as well as the Eucharist. They have also, over the years, become an important part of Anglican spirituality.

What of the Future?

In this chapter, we have been taking a look at some of the historical roots of our Anglican worship. We have seen how, from these, have grown both the traditional *Book of Common Prayer* and the recent *Book of Alternative Services*. As this is being written, the former remains the official Prayer Book of the Anglican Church of Canada, yet it is clear that, at some point in the future, there will be a new Prayer Book and that, in essence, it will be *the Book of Alternative Services*. While it remains strictly an alternative book, there is the opportunity for further change and revision which will certainly be made before the final version takes shape. At some stage, this will come before General Synod which will then have to decide upon the book to serve the worshipping needs of the turn of the century.

4

Disciplined
for Action

Up to this point, we have been thinking of how we begin and
then continue to grow in the Christian life. In Chapter 1 and
again when we were considering baptism, we looked at the
twofold process in which we receive Jesus as Saviour and are
filled and empowered by the Spirit of God. We have thought
about how we can grow in the new life through prayer and Bible
study, the sacraments, and worship with our fellow Christians.
But, so far, we have not looked at where all this is leading. In
this chapter we shall go one step further as we consider what it
means to be a changed person, and what implications this has
for our lives both within the church and the wider community.

The diagram on the following page will give an indication of
the scope of this chapter, and will serve as a guide to the different sections that follow.

A Guided by Rule

Once we have received Jesus as our Saviour and accepted the gift
of the Holy Spirit into our life, we are set upon a new path. As we
have seen, this is central to our understanding of what it means
to be a Christian. We have a clear direction to follow and new
power for living. But, in order that we might be kept moving
along this new path, and make all the new power effectively
coordinated, we need to have some guidelines. Such guidelines
have traditionally been called a rule of life, an organized way of
going about all the things that enrich our life in Christ. They are
a means of ensuring that we are living as properly balanced
Christians.

A rule of life will normally consist of five or six simple promises that we make to God and do our best to keep. Here are the
most common things we shall want to include:

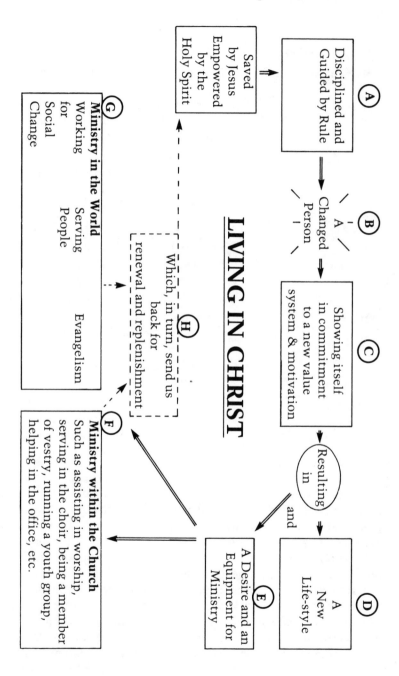

LIVING IN CHRIST

(A) Disciplined and Guided by Rule

→ Saved by Jesus Empowered by the Holy Spirit

(B) Changed Person ⇒

(C) Showing itself in commitment to a new value system & motivation

(D) A New Life-style

Resulting in and

(E) A Desire and an Equipment for Ministry

(F) **Ministry within the Church**
Such as assisting in worship, serving in the choir, being a member of vestry, running a youth group, helping in the office, etc.

(G) **Ministry in the World**
Working for Social Change   Serving People   Evangelism

(H) Which, in turn, send us back for renewal and replenishment

Prayer:	How often? For how long?
Bible Reading/Meditation:	Daily? Two or three times a week?
Holy Communion:	Note that the rule of the church is once a week on the Lord's Day. Perhaps you might want to promise to make your communion once *during* the week as well?
Confession:	If you decide that you want to use this means of strength, you might wish to make your confession quarterly, monthly?
Retreat:	Once a year, with perhaps a quiet day as well?
Fellowship:	Participation in some kind of sharing or praying group. How frequently?
Service:	We are told in the Bible that love should express itself in action. This might take the form of active service in the church or local community.
Almsgiving:	We are to share our wealth in the service of God. The biblical tithe is 10% of our income. The Anglican Church suggests 5% as a start.

These are examples of some of the things you might wish to include in your rule. This set of promises should be both realistic and prayerful. It should not aim too high nor too low — it should be geared to what we might reasonably expect to achieve. It is not a test of how good we are, nor a means of winning God's favour. These are things we do — and want to do well — simply because we love God so much. Thus, when we do not achieve our promises, it does not mean we have failed; it means we were simply shooting too high, and the rule needs revising. Each person's rule is a very personal affair, but it is always advisable to talk about it with someone else — perhaps your priest, or a person you trust within the Christian community — before you make any final decisions. Living by rule helps the Holy Spirit flow more powerfully and creatively through us so that, more and more, we shall become renewed people.

B A Changed Person

This change begins the very moment that we receive God into our life, and it continues and develops as we make use of all the gifts that God gives us. The ultimate aim is that we should be *changed*. Saint Paul described the Christian as a "new creation" (2 Cor. 5.17). Christianity, in fact, is about all things "becoming new" (Rev. 21.5); it is a Gospel of radical change. So we should *expect* to become changed people.

Practising Christians certainly discover a new, inner sense of peace and wholeness. People whose lives have been changed by the Holy Spirit always witness to the new sense of joy and love in their lives, and others who know them remark on the change which has taken place. Fear and impotence are replaced by a sense of love which "casts out all fear" (1 John 4.18), and an assurance that with God all things really are possible. Prayer ceases to be a dull duty; it becomes a joyful reunion with God, and a powerful weapon to be treated with awe and respect.

C A New Value System — A New Motivation

But the change does not, and must not, stop here. If it does, then our religion is in severe danger of remaining mere pietism, open to the charge that we are only interested in "what God can do for me." If we allow the Holy Spirit to flow into our minds, deal with our prejudices, and inspire our wills, much more will happen. Our whole outlook on life will change in the most radical way; we shall come to see the world through new glasses. In fact, we shall come to see it as God himself does. We shall view the world in its full potential for good and creativity, and we will know the full horror of sin. We will be deeply motivated to act decisively. With our newly-opened eyes we shall come to look upon society with the love of God. What's more, it will become clear to us that a love which does not *act* is not real love at all. We shall learn what Saint John was talking about in his First Letter in the Bible. (See especially 1 John 2.7–11.)

As men and women who have grown up in the West, we have come to accept all the values of our world as if they were right and normal. We are conditioned by what our friends and neighbours think is right or wrong, and we learn to accept those judgements, usually without question. Just as a Russian is brought up to assume that capitalism is the root of all evil, so the average North American almost worships it like a god. If you are a construction worker living exclusively among working people, then you assume without question that unions are God's gift to society. But if you are a plant manager, moving exclusively in middle class circles, then you will regard them as little short of devilish! Most of our values and attitudes are determined by the social group we live in, and reinforced by the ads we watch on television and the newspapers we choose to read. Inevitably we accept the values we are fed, often without realizing that many of them are dangerous and destructive. The belief that stockpiling immense arsenals of nuclear weapons is the only form of defence, leads to the obscenity of one country's spending over $100 billion on armaments alone — an amount that could otherwise easily solve the world's hunger problem. Other examples are less dramatic but equally telling.

One of the chief results of Bible study, prayer, and discussion with our fellow Christians is that many of our assumptions about the world we live in will be questioned, and we shall learn to bring all things under the Word of God. This means that we shall learn to discern a rich vein of values running throughout the Bible, culminating in those we learn from the life and teaching of Christ himself. We shall learn to apply these values to our daily lives, and to the continual flow of events in the world. This will not only come about through discussion; it will also be informed and moulded by prayer, as we learn to bring all kinds of issues and questions to God and to our fellow Christians in prayer for guidance. It is amazing how our attitudes to war, business, violence, family life, education, welfare, and a thousand other things can change when we bring them openly to Christ. In this way, our values change. As God's love works in us, we are motivated to see that God's kingdom is indeed enabled to come here on earth, and that *his* will shall be done.

D　A New Life-style

This change in our attitudes and motivation will have many effects. One of them will be in our personal life-style. As we begin to see the self-centredness of our present style of living and the detrimental effect it so often has on others, we shall be motivated to change so that we live more in accordance with Christian values.

Here is a simple example. The life-style of most Christians is remarkably selfish. We can be partly excused for this because television ads tell us repeatedly that self-satisfaction is to be desired above all else in life, and that it is to be achieved above all else by gaining possessions. So we learn that to be happy, successful, and wanted, we have to smell like a pine tree, look like a painted doll, cover ourselves with fatty tissue, and add tons of pollution to the air every day! Yet our Christian values compel us to ask whether such self-gratification is tolerable. We will be forced to ask what our life-style is doing to us, what it is doing to other people (whose lives are perhaps being affected by the need to produce those goods we demand), and what the effect is upon our physical environment. Does our chosen life-style enhance or destroy the quality of our lives and that of others?

If our answer is negative, our new insights will necessarily lead to a change in our personal life-style. We shall want to lead simpler, less demanding, and less consuming lives, with a deeper sensitivity to the effects our actions have on those around us.

E　The Desire and Equipment for Ministry

When the Holy Spirit of God is poured out on us, we receive particular gifts for ministry. Read what Saint Paul says in his letters to the Corinthians (1 Corinthians 12) and the Ephesians (Ephesians 4). He lists a number of such gifts — prophecy, administration, interpretation, discernment, teaching, evangelism — but the list could be extended to include many others. The important point is that none of these gifts is given to anyone for his own benefit or exclusive use. They are all given for one end, namely, "the building up of the Body of Christ in love . . . for service" (Ephesians 4.12). We are reminded that Jesus did not leave the church behind in the world for the mutual enjoyment of its members. He created, commissioned, and empowered it to carry on his work of inaugurating the kingdom. That is why he taught his followers to pray "Thy kingdom come. Thy will be done, on earth . . ." (Matthew 6.10).

His church — and all its members — is commissioned for a purpose, and so each of us is given one or more gifts to do this work. Mark Gibbs wrote a book twenty years ago entitled *God's Frozen People*[12] in which he pictured the church as it so often is — a group of paralysed people, passive recipients of the ministry performed by a few ordained clergy. In contrast, he painted a picture of the church as God wills it and has empowered it to be — a vast army of people, all on active service, each with his or her own ministry to perform. This has been the theme of much more recent contemporary writing, a good example of which is Michael Harper's *Let My People Grow*.[13] It is crucial to realize that our commitment to Jesus will lead us into an active ministry, for which we are each uniquely equipped by special gifts of the Holy Spirit.

F   Ministry Within the Church

This ministry will probably be most obvious within the church itself, and it is here that the gifts mentioned by Saint Paul are chiefly exemplified. There is no doubt that the model of the local church described by Mark Gibbs has become less typical than it was twenty years ago. Lay people are becoming increasingly involved in the life and work of their congregations, and no longer is the rector the sole arbiter of all that goes on in the parish. But this is still far removed from the model of the local Christian parishes described in the Epistles, where the emphasis was upon a community within which everyone played a part. And so Saint Paul speaks of educators and administrators, of pastors and healers, of prophets and interpreters, of leaders in worship and speakers in tongues. In worship, nurture, maintenance, education, evangelism, and outreach of each community, all were participants.

And so today new models are being tried in order to harness these diverse gifts for the work of God in each Christian community. Harper describes one such experiment in north London, England, where team ministry in the parish consists of about ten people, only two of whom are ordained. The others are all lay people, committed to a full and active ministry in their local church. Their program extends far beyond the rôle of the usual church vestry or council member, and it also releases Harper to fulfill his calling as an evangelist in the wider church. Each Christian should examine himself to see what particular ministry God has given him to fulfill, and seek guidance as to how best it may be expressed in the local church.

G Ministry in the World

Here we are venturing into less secure territory, where the traditional guidelines are not nearly as sharply drawn. Everyone would agree that the changed and empowered Christian, just as much as the local church, should be reaching out in some way to the world. Moreover, there is no doubt that our Lord did not just tell us to be good Christians in church on Sundays — he sent us out to do his work from Monday to Saturday as well. The problem is to discern just what this commission means. I propose three categories which may help to clarify what it means to be a minister of Christ in the world.

1 In Evangelism. Evangelism is a much abused word, and its sister word "evangelical" has unfortunately become used to describe a particular wing of the church which suggests that only evangelicals are interested in evangelism. This, of course, is nonsense. The Christian church is by its very nature and commissioning evangelical — we are charged with the telling of the good news of Jesus Christ, of the release of the Holy Spirit, and of the implication of all this for the world. That sounds like, and is, a vast undertaking, but nonetheless, it is our task. Every Christian is meant to be an evangelist.

Now this does not mean that we have to conform to the image of the typical professional evangelist of American tradition. That is only one very narrow style of evangelism. The Word is far wider in its meaning. Instead, each of us is commissioned to witness to Christ in our daily lives. This witness may take many forms; it may mean standing up vocally for our beliefs in discussion, or testifying to the power of Christ in our own lives. Far too many of us certainly have a tendency to duck this! Evangelism may equally be shown by the basic quality or self-

lessness of our daily lives. I am sure that Mother Teresa has con-
verted more people to Christ by the example of her selfless love
for the unlovable of Calcutta than have most evangelists with
all the words at their command.[14] People should be able to see
Christ in the lives of those who call themselves Christians. If
we wonder what evangelism means, we might begin by asking
how our personal lives (our actions, our attitudes, our character
as well as our words) reflect Christ. *Do others see Christ in us?*

Yet the more articulate kind of evangelism still remains vital.
Many of us are critical of the door-to-door techniques of the
Mormons and Jehovah's Witnesses, but perhaps we ought to
consider whether our usual practice of doing nothing is any
better. It is important that these kinds of questions be discussed
in every parish by a group of concerned lay people with their
priest.

2   Serving People. Outreach cannot stop short at what we traditionally mean by evangelism. The Christian is one who is filled
with the love of God, and if that infilling is genuine, it will compel him to share that love with everyone — especially with
those who are unloved. The Bible is nowhere more powerful
than when it turns to this theme. Saint John tells us that "if a
man says he loves God but does not love his brother" (1 John
3.17), then that person's Christianity is fraudulent. What are
the implications of true love? The parable of Jesus leaves us in
no doubt. Having outlined the needs of the hungry, the poor, the
sick, the prisoner, Jesus went on: "In that you have not loved
the least of these my brethren, you have not loved me" (Matthew 25.40). Love means caring for our fellow human beings,
and especially for the poor, the sick, and the powerless — all
those whom the rest of the world customarily dismisses with
contempt. These, before all others, we are to love. And we are to
love them by *serving* them, not by patronizing them with the in-
sufferably hypocritical attitude of munificent benefactors. We
are to identify ourselves with them, just as Jesus himself came
to live and mingle with the unwanted people of his own day.
The contemporary term is "solidarity."

The Christian will therefore seek the greatest need, the
greatest suffering, the worst degree of dehumanization, and see
how best he or she can serve Christ there. This has been the

inspiration for all genuine Christian social service, from the Little Sisters of Charity to the present day "meals on wheels" operations. We can all make lists of the kind of things that we can envision ourselves being part of. Here are a few: helping to man a suicide line, regularly visiting old or shut-in people, helping to renovate old or poor housing, baby-sitting so a single parent can have a night out, raising funds for a particular need, shopping for a sick person, helping to staff a boys' or girls' club, giving lessons on housekeeping to retarded adults, and so on. We can all dream, but the important thing is to pitch in and stick at it — for the love of God!

3 Working for Social Change. Here is the tricky area where many of us are scared off because it invariably seems to lead into politics. And of course, it frequently does. But we need to remember that the word *politics* simply refers to the way we choose to organize our corporate life together. If we are concerned about improving the quality of this life, then inevitably we are into politics. So I would make no apology for the use of this word.

Perhaps it would be helpful if we were to define a base on which to establish ourselves before we go any further, to save the frequent misunderstanding that often arises in this area. This base is very clearly given to us in the Bible. One of the most lasting contributions of the great prophets (Amos, Isaiah, Jeremiah, etc.) was that they would not let the rulers of their day get away with separating religion and daily life into two water-tight compartments. God was just as concerned about people's living conditions as he was about any amount of religious activity. He cared that men should not swindle their neighbour, cheat widows, or exploit the poor; such things were an abomination and would surely lead to disaster. God was as much concerned about business, commerce, politics, and industry as he was about the number of bulls sacrificed in the temple — indeed, infinitely more so! (See especially Amos 5.10 ff., Isaiah 1.10 ff., and Jeremiah 7.5 ff.)

This message was taken up and reinforced by Jesus, who roundly attacked the profiteers and sharp business people of his day, any in fact who were living off the backs of others. And the signs of the kingdom which he came to announce were the proclamation of good news for the poor, freedom for the oppressed, and liberty for captives (Luke 4.18). He led people to pray and work for a new kingdom, a renewed society, in which each would have his daily bread. His impending birth was greeted with a song by Mary. Her words announced the overthrow of the rich and the powerful, and the raising of the poor (Luke 1.46–55). In other words, Jesus was concerned with radical change in the world.

Now it is important to note that this social concern is not to be confused with mere political revolution, which is so frequently the substitution of one kind of oppression for another. Yet a change is demanded, and its shape is made clear when we substitute a Christian value system for that of the world in which we live. Thus, a Christian is bound to work for a society whose systems are geared not to exploit the poor for the sake of a limited number of rich people, but to ensure that every man and woman and child should have sufficient to live on. A truly Christian political system will enable each individual to have the greatest possible measure of freedom commensurate with the freedom of others. Our society should be geared to ends that are personal and social rather than technological or economic, so that each person may achieve the greatest possible fulness of life. We need to remember that Jesus came to bring such fulness to us.

The Christian is therefore committed to working for the kingdom of God in the world or, to put it another way, a substitution of his way for ours. One hallmark of this would be to see the needs of all people regarded equally. But the implications of this way of thinking are not often easy. It implies that every Christian should become a worker for a better world, to change it from its present, sorry, and misguided state. This is why we talk of working for social change.

This action will take a great variety of forms, depending upon the issues we perceive, and the position we might happen to hold in society. For example, we might be concerned about dispossessed farmers in South America, tenants who are being forced out of their homes in a nearby apartment block, or a new highway which threatens to destroy an inner city housing area. We may be concerned about reforming our prison system, doing something about the high cost of food, or protesting the amount of violence on television.

Am I a business executive, a housewife, a school teacher, a student at college or a retired railway man? How much am I influenced in my attitudes by self-interest or by the prejudices of my friends and colleagues? What biblical and Christian insights and values can I perceive which may help me come to a truly Christian viewpoint about the issues before me? These are some of the questions that we will, and should, find ourselves asking.

But then, what can we do? This is a question that often frustrates us, and forces many of us into total paralysis. It is so easy today to feel helpless in the face of the many powerful forces which are stronger than ourselves. When we hear of the most appalling suffering in Cambodia or hunger in the Sahel, we say, "What can *I* do?" When we are faced with what many see as a frightening prospect of nuclear war and confrontation by the year 2000, we are tempted to give up hope or lapse into a religion of personal piety which excuses us from facing up to such issues. Yet it is important that we do not give up hope or stick our heads into the sand of religious pietism. Whatever our position in society, there is always something we can do. I have drawn the following diagram in the hope that it may help us to see some way in which we can use our personal freedom to accomplish something. It shows how every action is related and is part of a larger pattern. The implication is that when I say my prayers, send my cheque, or take part in a protest march, my actions are not solitary. They are part of a whole pattern of action that thousands of other Christians are taking. So we should not despair that our small action is not moving the mountain of world poverty and hunger. Our faithful effort, together with the response of thousands and even millions of others, will move even the biggest of mountains.

The diagram is very simple. It clarifies a wide variety of actions which we might take with respect to any particular issue. On the left of the central line are actions in which we can engage as a group — perhaps as a parish or house group. On the right are actions we might take as individuals.

On the top of the diagram, you will find the words *hard action* and at the bottom *soft action*. The former I would define as those that are highly challenging; they include greater risk to reputation, and possibly to our person. The soft actions are less demanding and usually more private. This does not mean to say

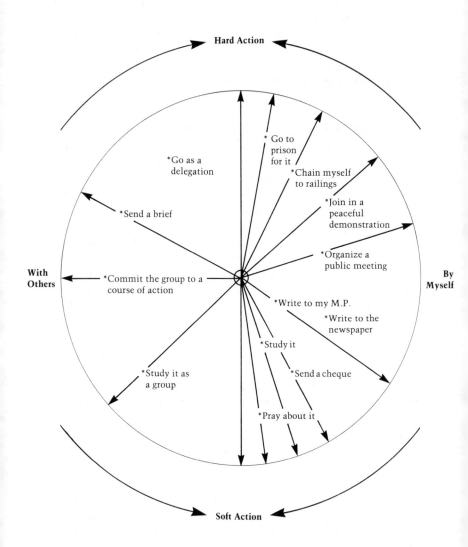

that they are less effective or important. Actions, whether on one's own or with others, must thus be graded on a scale from "hard" to "soft."

An example of one particular action might be helpful. In Montreal, a few years ago, there was a movement for the reduction of fares for senior citizens on the city's public transit system. Many people in the city were concerned about this, and many in the churches felt this was something they should strongly support. Yet there was complete opposition from city hall. A considerable number of Christians therefore became involved in a variety of ways. As "soft" actions, we prayed about it in our churches and privately as individuals. Some wrote to their councillors, others to the city papers. Those who knew people in city hall did what they could to lobby for a change in the fare structure.

Some people opted for "harder" actions. They took part in a peaceful demonstration by senior citizens and stood at the transit stops, handing out pamphlets and collecting signatures for a petition. Some of the seniors even went so far as to ride the buses while refusing to pay. In the end, the message was heard. Each person had played his or her part; prayers, letters, marches, and defiant actions achieved their end: the fares were reduced.

All issues are not so simple or clear-cut as this one, yet it does illustrate ways in which Christians are able to serve God by working for an improved society. It also shows that there are many ways of doing it. What is needed is faith, imagination, and the kind of love that is not afraid to take risks.

H   Back to God

The cycle is complete. Having been commissioned and empowered by God, we have become changed persons. This is reinforced and encouraged as we do our best to follow a rule of life, so that we are fed by the Word of God, the sacraments of the church, and the fellowship of our brother and sister Christians. This will result in an altered attitude toward life, manifesting itself in a changed system of values, and a new sense of motivation.

In turn, this leads not only to a transformation of our personal life-style, but also to a desire to serve God whenever and wherever we can. Moreover, the outpouring of the Holy Spirit in our life brings with it particular gifts which are to be used in his service. As Jesus himself told us, this means service to our fellow human beings, and particularly to those whom the world counts as of little value. This ministry is to be partially worked out within the church itself, in love and service to our fellow Christians; but it is equally to be focused on the world outside, on the wider community of which we are all part. As we seek the opportunities to serve the needs of others and the challenge to change the world, the wheel comes around full circle. We will feel the need for all the resources that God has to give us; we shall return, hungry for communion with God and our fellow Christians, searching for enlightenment and direction from the reading of his Word, impatient to know and be renewed by him in our prayer. And so we shall come back to the God who died and rose for us, and to the Holy Spirit who washes and refreshes us in his waters. And in this, God is seen to be glorified.

Understanding
Our
Faith

5

The Old Testament

One of the first things to remember about the Christian faith is that it is rooted in history. It is all about a God who has made himself known to us through a series of historical events, climaxing in the historical birth, death, and resurrection of Jesus of Nazareth. In order to understand our faith, we need to know about these events; we need to discover our roots in the Bible. The New Testament tells the story of Jesus and the earliest days of the Christian church, while the Old Testament is the record of the two thousand years of history leading up to these events. Any Christian who wants to understand his faith must begin with these primary sources.

We start with the Old Testament. What kind of text is it? It is not a single book, but rather a whole library of books, each one separately written (and often rewritten) during the thousand years of history before the birth of Jesus. The Bible, in other words, is a collection of books, bound together because they all have something in common — together they tell the story of God's people.

Like other collections, the Bible contains a wide variety of literary forms and styles. There is plain, straightforward *history*, such as the First Book of Kings, which tells of the days of the great King David in about the year 1,000 B.C. There is *mythology*, in which the story of the creation of the world and the fallen nature of mankind is described, as in the first few chapters of Genesis. Also in that particular book are *legends*, handed down by generations of storytellers, such as those that tell of the founding of ancient wells in the desert land. Sometimes we come upon *law codes*, not unlike those that were written by other great nations of the world. Some of these codes, like the Ten Commandments, were relatively old, going back to the days before Israel's final entry into the promised land. Other, such as those in Leviticus, were written much later. They reflect an age when Israel had experienced exile, and when professional lawmakers had begun to create an increasingly elaborate legal system.

There is a great deal of *poetry*, reflecting the fact that much of the material in the Bible was passed on by word of mouth long before it was written down, for it is always easier to remember poetry than prose. The "Song of Deborah" (Judges 5) is probably the earliest poetry of the Old Testament, recording the somewhat violent exploits of a Hebrew woman during the reconquest of Palestine under Joshua. The poetry of the Old Testament is infinitely varied, from the love poems of the Song of Songs to the laments of the Jewish people in exile from their homeland (Lamentations); from the vengeful war poetry of Habbakuk to the intensely personal outpourings of many of the psalms. The Book of Psalms forms a complete collection of poetry and song, written over some six hundred years. The individual psalms express the full gamut of very personal human emotions, as well as the joys and sorrows of the nation in times of national celebration and penitence. They were, in fact, the hymns of the Jewish people.

There are also collections of *wisdom sayings*, a form of literature far more common then than today. In a pre-literary age, people learned wise sayings which, as they were memorized and passed on, played an important part in moulding a people's character and shaping their conduct. Jews took pride in remembering and quoting such proverbs, just as I can well remember my own grandfather doing so many years ago.

One of the best known forms of literature in the Old Testament is the writings of the greater and lesser *prophets*. This description is not always quite accurate, because the prophets were not primarily writers, but men who spoke out as they felt inspired by God. What we have now in the prophetic books is sometimes their written words, but much more often we find sayings that were collected and then written down by their followers. In this way, the secretary Baruch recorded the prophecies of his master Jeremiah, and we have him to thank for this vitally important record.

The prophets were not strictly foretellers of history, although sometimes they did make historical forecasts. They were primarily men who had a special ability to discern the mind of

God in particular historical situations. They were inspired. The prophet Amos, for example, proclaimed that the law of God had social implications, which forbade the exploitation of the weak. In a similar fashion the politically conscious Isaiah protested forcibly against the royal policy of relying upon Egyptian arms, rather than God, for support.

Another kind of biblical literature is known as *apocalyptic* writing. This is extremely difficult for us to understand because there is simply no modern equivalent. *Apocalypse* implies the "breaking in" of God into history; it is concerned with the end of the world both in the sense of time and of purpose. It employs language full of symbols and imagery. It might help to think of apocalyptic writing as mythology, not of the past, but of the future. The great danger we encounter when reading this kind of material today is that we take its meaning too literally rather than listening to the underlying message, be it one of triumph or doom. The Book of Revelation contains some good examples of this kind of writing, but we need knowledge of the background and the style of this literary form to be able to interpret it.

The Old Testament, then, is not a single book but a whole collection of books containing within them a wide and varied selection of literature. What holds the Old Testament together?

The superficial answer is that at a certain time in history (approximately eighty years after Jesus), a decision was made by the Jews to recognize a certain number of books as the "Scriptures," a collection of writings believed to be inspired by God, and therefore having special authority. Many other writings of undoubted religious value were written after this date, but they were not recognized as part of the "canon" of the Jewish Scriptures. Later on, the Christian church simply accepted this official collection, calling it the "Old Testament" to distinguish it from the "New Testament" or "covenant," which God had made through Jesus Christ.

But why did the Jews draw the line at this *particular* collection of books, choosing not to include others? What was it that they all had in common? The answer is quite simple. They were held together by a single theme: they all described the ongoing relationship of the Lord with the Jews, his people, from the earliest days of their recorded history. One could say that they tell the story of God's gradual revelation of himself (his character, his will) to his chosen people over some 2,000 years. Or the Old Testament could be described as a record of the gradual discovery of what God was like. Through the events and experiences, the heady joys and bitter sorrows of two thousand years, the Jewish people came to know their God — and the story of their experience and the essence of what they discovered is contained in those pages.

If the reader has not already read a history of Israel, I would strongly recommend doing so to underpin what I have to say now. What follows is not the whole story but a short scenario, including the main themes, of how the rough, tribal religion of the people of Abraham slowly grew into the spiritually sophisticated faith of the prophetic and priestly traditions in the years before Jesus.

Beginnings: Abraham, the Founder of the People (c. 1850 B.C.)

The story begins with Abraham. He was not a mythical creation, but the fact that his name means "tribal father" suggests that the memories of him may well have been enhanced over the centuries. Sometime during the second century of the second millenium before Christ (see chart), Abraham led his people from the fertile lands of Mesopotamia (modern Iran) into the north of Palestine. With this exploit, the story begins.

It continues over a period of perhaps three hundred years with the stories of the patriarchs — characters who have come down to us as Isaac, Jacob, Esau, and Joseph, together with other reputed founders of the various clans of those early Jewish settlers. How much history and legend is mixed up in these early stories, it is impossible to say, but we can get a vivid picture of the early life and wanderings of these ancient nomads as they slowly settled the land.[15]

These people thought of God as a wrathful and unpredictable tribal deity. Just as every other tribe or nation had their own tribal or national gods, this Lord was *their* Lord. If the Jews thought of their God as being more powerful (which they soon came to do), they also recognized that the other gods were also potent. Their God could be not only powerful but vindictive. On occasion, he could demand human sacrifice. Abraham did not relish the idea of killing his only son Isaac as a sacrifice on

Date	Events	Literature	Important Themes
1850 (approx.)	Abraham leads Hebrews into Palestine The "patriarchial" period.		God's promise to his people.
1600 (approx.)	Hebrews settle in Egypt.	Period of purely oral tradition.	
1250 (approx.)	Exodus from Egypt under Moses. Beginning of settlement in Palestine. Time of the judges.		Moses is given the law.
1000	David King of united Israel. The nation is divided into Israel (north) & Judah (south).	1st editions of historical writings. i.e. Samuel & Kings.	Period of the great prophets.
741	The fall of Samaria: north kingdom destroyed.	Amos, Hosea, 1st Isaiah. Deuteronomy.	The law is reformed.
597 & 586	Jerusalem destroyed. Jews exiled into Babylon.	Jeremiah. Ezekiel	
535	Babylon defeated by Persians. Jews allowed to return home. Rebuilding of the city, the temple & the religion.	Nehemiah — Ezra	Growing importance of the law and the temple.
349	Greek invasion: from now on ruled by Greeks.	Daniel	
61	Romans enter Jerusalem: Roman rule begins.		Growing hope for deliverance.

the primitive altar, but he never doubted that it was quite proper for God to make such a demand (Genesis 22). One point about Abraham's understanding stood out; clearly God wanted a *special* relationship with Israel. There was already a tight bond between them, a special covenant. This was symbolized by the rainbow in Genesis (Genesis 9.12), and clearly expressed in two strictly enforced laws: (i) no Israelite was to marry outside his tribe — so Isaac had to journey all the way back to his ancestral home in order to find himself a wife — and (ii) no Israelite was to worship any other god — this was absolutely forbidden. The second law was stated repeatedly.

The Covenant

The idea of the covenant was the foundation of the Jewish understanding of their God. It expressed the special relationship that the Lord had with his chosen people. From this understanding the Hebrews derived the strong sense of their unique identity, as well as those concepts of morality, obedience, and accountability that were to characterize their faith.

After some three hundred years of settlement as nomads in Palestine, a large number of the Hebrew people migrated into Egypt as a part of a general movement of Semitic nomads (called the Hyksos peoples) about the year 1600 B.C. This may well have been due to the pressure of famine, as the story of Joseph in Genesis (chapters 37–50), so graphically describes. Regardless of the precise historical details of this story, it is generally agreed that the Hebrew migration took place at this time, when the reigning Hyksos Pharaoh of Egypt was disposed to welcome a group of fellow Semites into the country. A large group of Hebrews settled peacefully in Egypt for several generations.

About the year 1250 B.C., there was a dynastic revolution in Egypt, and the pro-Hebrew royal house was overthrown. The successor, Ramses II, was not so kindly toward the Hebrews. He was a prolific builder of prestigious buildings, and saw in the Hebrew settlers a convenient supply of slave labour.

Moses, the child of a Hebrew slave, had grown up in the royal household. After killing an Egyptian slave-guard, Moses escaped and was sheltered by a nomadic tribe who grazed their flocks near Mount Sinai, across the Nile and to the east. One day, he had a vivid experience of God calling him to go back to Egypt and lead his people out of slavery. Through a series of heroic exploits, including escape from the pursuing Egyptian army at the "Reed" Sea, he succeeded in bringing a crowd of refugees into the land of Sinai, where the single most important event in Jewish history took place.

In a series of awesome encounters with God on the holy mountain, a covenant was formally and ritually contracted between God and his people. This was to be the foundation of all subsequent Jewish history, and its terms are to be found in the present books of Exodus and Deuteronomy.

In effect, God's message was this: "You obey me and I'll look after you; but, if you disobey my commands, then watch out!" There followed a whole series of laws which his people were to keep. This is why "the law" has ever since been at the heart of the Jewish faith.

Question: "How am I to be assured of the Lord's favour?"
Answer: "By obedience to the Lord."
Question: "But how am I to obey the Lord?"
Answer: "By following the law."

It was as straightforward as that. To follow the commandments of the law would assure one of God's protection and favour. God would restore to the Jews their ancestral lands, protect them from their enemies, and give them peace and prosperity. But if the people should deviate from the law, putting their trust in another God or in their own strength rather than the Lord's, then he would use natural calamities or even the power of other nations to show them that he was indeed their God!

Heroes and Kings (c. 1250–950 B.C.)

All that followed was interpreted according to this dictum: leaders and individuals were judged by whether or not they obeyed the commandments of God. The ebb and flow of events was seen as an expression of God's pleasure at his people's obedience, or his wrath at their stubbornness. Yet, all the time, their understanding of God and his character was growing deeper.

Following Moses' death, the people again entered Palestine (1250 B.C. approx. onward), gradually occupying the land and inevitably encountering those who already lived there. Most important, they met the Philistines, colonists from Cyprus, who had settled the coastal region and opposed the expanding Israelites. In a series of sporadic guerilla campaigns, various leaders (or "judges") — such as Jephthah, Gideon, and Samson — pushed these peoples back until a way was opened for all the separate tribes to be united under one national leader.

Saul was the first king of the Israelites, and under his successor

David, Israel became the most powerful country among its neighbours. Evidence of this power was born out when, in the subsequent reign of King Solomon, the Ethiopian Queen of Sheba came all the way from her distant country to show her allegiance. This period of national strength reached its peak about one thousand years before Christ. This is why the Jewish people have always looked back to King David with such great nostalgia. David himself, although not without his human faults, was regarded as one who had been faithful to his God; and so it was that his reign and that of his son, Solomon, prospered.

Disintegration of the Nation — A Deepening Understanding of God (c. 950 B.C. onward)

In the centuries that followed this political highpoint of Jewish history, we can trace two developments. On the one hand, political affairs slowly went from bad to worse. But, on the other hand, the Jews' understanding of their God deepened, probably as a result of their hardship. The thousand years of history after King David's rule saw the disintegration of the united kingdom into the separate nations of Israel in the north and Judah in the south. The total destruction of Israel and the defeat and exile of Judah also took place during this time. And, even after their return from exile, it was not long before Judah was overrun and occupied first by the Greeks and then by the Romans. Here is a brief outline of that disintegration.

1000 B.C. United kingdom under Saul, David, and Solomon.
   931 On the death of Solomon, his rivals divide the kingdom into Israel (north) and Judah (south).
   741 Total destruction of the northern kingdom.
   597 Destruction of southern kingdom and the exile of
   586 its peoples into Babylon.
   535 The return of the exiles from Babylon to Jerusalem.
   323 Defeat and occupation by the Greeks.
    61 Defeat and occupation by the Romans.

On the death of King Solomon in 931, there was a dispute about who should follow him on the throne of the united kingdom. The north favoured one claimant and the south another. As a result, the kingdom was divided. For two hundred years, they continued side by side under separate kings. During the middle of the eighth century, their north-eastern neighbour, Assyria, began to grow powerful and sought to extend its power over the whole of the Palestine. In the series of conflicts that followed, the Israelite city of Samaria was totally destroyed and from then on the northern kingdom ceased to exist. Her people were killed or taken away into permanent slavery, and the land was resettled by other conquered peoples. Subsequently the Jews to the south ceased to regard their northern neighbours as fellow Jews, and the name "Samaritan" became a term of scorn.

Judah survived the threat of Assyria and eventually the Assyrian Empire collapsed under the growing power of Babylon (the modern state of Iran). The Babylonians, like their conquered predecessors, sought to impose their will on the surrounding peoples, and they demanded subservience from Judah. When Judah refused, the Babylonians overran the country, first in 597 and again ten years later, each time capturing Jerusalem. In 586, they transported most of its inhabitants to Babylon, and the city fell into ruin.

Fifty years later (in 535 B.C.), the wheel of history turned again. Babylon was, in its turn, overthrown by the rising power of Persia. The conquering King Cyrus issued a decree authorizing the Jewish people to return to their homeland, and so they returned to rebuild their city and their religion. Here they remained until the time of our Lord, but rarely were they their own masters. In 349, Alexander of Macedon began his incredible march of conquest which was to lead from Greece to the Indus River, and eventually resulted in the creation of the Greek Empire.

Judah was one of the countries to be crushed by the Greek army on its march eastward and, after the death of Alexander, it came to be ruled by the Greek house of Seleucid. For nearly three hundred years, the Jewish people chafed under Greek rule; they constantly threatened rebellion and finally, under the leadership of the Maccabee family, seized control of their country and enjoyed a brief period of self rule. But in 61 B.C., with the old Greek Empire crumbling into ruins before the might of the new Roman Empire, the Roman general Vespasian entered Jerusalem and the country passed to the rule of Rome. It remained under Roman rule until further revolts in A.D. 70 and

140, when Jerusalem was destroyed, and the Jewish people were exiled from their homeland.

The Prophets

The story of the Jews was one of almost continuous political disaster, yet through all the years of turmoil their religion was steadily refined and toughened. One of the most important of all phenomena during the centuries immediately following the division of the kingdom was the appearance of the prophets. We have already seen how these men were not so much fore-tellers of the future as people who were gifted with special insight into the character of God and his will for his people. Above all, they were men regarded by their contemporaries as having been inspired and filled with the Spirit of God, as if God had entered into them, giving them divine insight and authority. Due to their gifts of insight, the character of God was slowly revealed.

Hosea (late 8th century B.C.), a man whose wife had repeatedly deserted him and run off after different lovers, realized how God must so often feel because Israel turned its back on him and followed other gods. His writing is a testimonial to divine compassion and God's readiness to accept his people back, even when they have forgotten or betrayed him.

Amos (mid 8th century B.C.) was a fiery shepherd from the northern hills who descended upon the city in a blaze of anger against the social injustices of his time. It might almost be said that he was one of the first men in history to see that God is concerned with social morality. God forbids us to oppress our fellow men and commands us to pursue justice.

The first of the three prophets to call himself **Isaiah** (responsible for chapters 1 to 39) was, in contrast to Amos, a sophisticated man of the court. He lived at a time of political and military crisis, when the Assyrian army was threatening to overrun and destroy Judah just as it had the northern kingdom (late 8th century). Set in the midst of national affairs, Isaiah saw that God was Lord, not only of the Jews, but of all men. In fact Isaiah was responsible for the major breakthrough in man's understanding of God: he proclaimed that there was only *one*

God. Isaiah was the first "monotheist," a believer in the one, universal deity. This was a dramatically new vision of God. The Jews now realized that their God also controlled the other nations as well, even though they continued to believe that he still had a special relationship with them.

Other prophets built upon these foundations and added new dimensions to the people's faith. **Jeremiah**, who lived to see the catastrophic destruction of Jerusalem by the Babylonians in 597 and 586, added the concept of individual responsibility. Until this time, the Jews had thought predominantly of the relationship between the whole people and their God. Jeremiah perceived that, to God, the individual was also important, and that men and women would be held accountable for their own individual sins.

The implications of such teachings were profound and, even before Jeremiah's time, attempts had been made to incorporate them into the Law. So it is recorded that, toward the close of the seventh century (about 626 B.C.), the good King Josiah formalized a book of such reformed laws and instituted sweeping changes in the life of Judah. He totally destroyed all the idolatrous hill shrines, killing their priests, and attempted to set up a "purified" religion in accordance with the newly discovered law-book. He also promulgated the new laws (the present book of Deuteronomy) and tried to see that they were observed. An example of this is the law that lays down the principle of "an eye for an eye." We now regard this as very harsh, but it merely asserted the principle that no punishment should be greater than the original crime. No one, for example, should lose his life simply for stealing a sheep. This was a remarkable step forward in respect for human life and personhood, and it was a direct result of the teachings of the greater prophets.

Two Important Effects of the Exile: The Law and the Temple

Two important developments which we see in the last few centuries before the birth of Christ have to do with the enhancement of the law and the temple. It was primarily the years in exile (586 to 535 B.C.) that led to these developments. Perhaps it will be helpful if we try to put ourselves in the position of a pious and devout Jew during those terrible years away from the homeland. We might read a chapter from Lamentations to imagine how a homesick Jew must have felt.

Yet for some Jews, there was even more to agonize over than mere homesickness. "How is it," they must have asked, "that this terrible disaster has come about? How can the Lord have allowed us, his own people, to be destroyed and to suffer in this way?" There could be only one answer: it must have been because they had broken their side of the Covenant — they had disobeyed the Law of the Lord. This had no doubt been due to wilful disobedience, but partly also to ignorance. Perhaps they had not always *known* when they were breaking the law, but one thing was now clear: they must never break it again.

This kind of obedience would require a knowledge of precisely what the law laid down in any given situation. When the exiles returned to their own country once more, it was with the conviction that the law had to be revised in order to make ignorance of it impossible. And so the law grew immensely, in importance and in detail. New, more precise laws were written, and even history was rewritten to leave their descendants in no doubt as to where they had gone wrong in the past. The laws of Leviticus were tabulated, and the book of Chronicles was written as a revised version of the events previously described in the book of Kings.

Something else also happened. The law was becoming increasingly complicated; it required more and more expert interpretation. Two new professions came into being: the *scribe*, whose job it was to write down the laws, and the *lawyer*, whose task it was to interpret them. Because humanity is inherently sinful, the scribe and the lawyer eventually came to enjoy and misuse their power so that, by Jesus' time, we find them particular objects of his wrath.

The other major development resulting from the exile was the growth of the *temple* and its priesthood in Jerusalem. Parallel with the expansion of the law was the growing importance of the temple cult, and the tradition of sacrificial offerings upon which a strong cult had grown. This business of sacrifices was nothing new in Israel's history. Sacrificial offerings went back into the mists of time, but there is no doubt that the temple cult received new impetus after the exile — and for the same reason that the law grew in importance. For the returning exiles, it was a matter of supreme importance to keep on the right side of God — they knew the consequences if they did not! One way of maintaining God's favour was by the meticulous following of the law; the other was by the equally meticulous observance of the temple ceremonies. And so it was that the temple cult grew, and the roles of the priests and their assistants (the Levites) increased. Inevitably, others cashed in on this. The money-changers traded ordinary money for "temple money" at a high rate of profit. Meanwhile, the trade in the temple courtyard encouraged others to exploit the thousands who came along to buy sheep or pigeons, which the law required to be offered by the priests.

Continued Political Disaster and Its Effects

As we saw, the return from exile did not lead to eternal peace and prosperity. After a period of relative calm during which the Jews were able to rebuild their shattered nation and its religion, there came the Greek and then the Roman invasions. Long years followed during which the Jewish people's bitterness and resentment against their oppressors steadily grew. The triumph of the Maccabeans restored some sense of national pride and hope, but the coming of Vespasian and the Roman legionaries in 61 B.C. dashed such hopes to the ground. When puppet kings and a Roman governor were set up to administer the old northern and southern kingdoms, the Jews realized that they had simply exchanged one foreign despot for another.

Through all these long years, it was inevitable that bitterness, nationalism, and religious questioning should find some outlet. Devout and pious Jews, in particular, were bound to feel bitter that things had gone so disastrously. Some felt angry and violent, some looked to arms for a way out, some to prayer and retreat, but they all clung to a hope that God would "do something." This faith expressed itself in the growth of a number of religious movements and in the emergence of a new hope.

Groups, Communities, and the Messianic Hope

One option was to turn to violence. God clearly could not want this oppression to continue. He simply needed an instrument to overthrow the oppressors. And so the terrorists chose themselves to be the instruments of God's wrath. They called themselves *"zealots."* Their method was much the same as that of the guerillas or terrorists of today, and they were responsible for a great deal of unrest and insurrection in our Lord's day.

Another approach was to retreat from the world entirely and resort to prayer and strict purity of living. Some of the most extreme groups who practised this were the *Essenes*, who retired from involvement in worldly affairs, led ascetic lives, and waited for God to intervene. One such group had its centre in the cliffs above the Dead Sea; their library was accidentally discovered by a shepherd boy in 1949.

A group which had something in common with the Essenes were the *Pharisees*, although they did not believe in retirement from the world. The Pharisees belonged to communities, and bound themselves to lead exemplary lives according to the commandments of the law. They believed that if people lived strictly by the law, then God would bring them deliverance. Inevitably, such an attitude tended to breed a hypocritical and "holier than thou" character, although the Pharisees were in fact held in marked respect by most people.

All of these groups, and many others, had grown up under the rule of the Greeks and the Romans. But still the oppression continued, and the question began to burn white-hot in their minds. "How long can God allow this to go on? Surely he will come and save us?" But how would he deliver his people?

The people remembered previous times of serious crisis when the Lord had raised up great leaders, heroes to their people. He would do so again. Such men had been great and successful, not because of their human abilities, but because God had endowed them with divine power. He had poured out his Spirit on them; he had "anointed" them (the Hebrew word for "anointed" is *Messiah* or in Greek, *Christos*).

A hope began to grow that God would act again, this time in an even more dramatic and decisive way than in the past. He would intervene in the course of human history; he would raise up one who would combine the roles of prophet, priest, and king, and would empower him with his Spirit. Such a leader would inaugurate a new era on the earth, an era which would be ruled, not by an emperor in Rome, but by God through his anointed one. A new kingdom of God was about to emerge; the end of the present order was at hand; the axe was laid to the root of the tree of Roman power (see Matthew 3.2 and 10.7). People were called upon to stand up and declare themselves — for God and his kingdom, or against him? Were they ready to give up their present life and risk all on the new order that was coming?

Here we have come to the banks of the Jordan River and are listening to the words of one who called himself John, the Baptist. The story of the old covenant is nearly at an end; a new covenant is about to be forged.

6

Jesus, the Leader Who Was Different

At this point in the drama, a new character steps onto the stage and a new era in history begins. A stranger from the northern village of Nazareth suddenly appears before John the Baptist on the bank of the Jordan River and asks to be baptized into this new kingdom. Accounts differ as to whether John knew exactly who Jesus was at this time — he was still uncertain some time later (see Matthew 11.1-6) — but the occasion undoubtedly marks the beginning of the public career of Jesus, who was later to be called the Messiah, or the Christ.

A Jesus the Man

Although the Gospels do not try to be biographies in the modern sense of the word, they do present us with all the material we need in order to put together a simple life of Jesus. Using them as our basic source, let us go back in time to about the year A.D. 33 and imagine that we are on the staff of the chief daily paper in Rome. There have been rumours that something odd has recently been happening in Jerusalem, a trouble spot which has repeatedly been in the news with its stories of terrorism and unrest. The Jews are a difficult and proud people. They have never taken kindly to the Roman occupation, and it does not take much to put a light to their smouldering hostility. In fact, recently the governor has been forced to execute a terrorist leader for instigating violence in the city.

But the new rumour has it that something much more intriguing is afoot. The followers of the executed man are insisting that he has reappeared after his burial and has commanded them to proclaim a new kingdom on earth. Even the Jews themselves are said to be upset. What is behind the story?

This is what we are sent to find out, but remember, the paper will print no unfounded rumours, just the plain, unadulterated facts. What follows now are the bare bones of the story which emerges after a number of interviews with many who claim to have known Jesus and witnessed what has taken place.

Jesus appears to have been born in a small town called Bethlehem, not very far from Jerusalem itself. His mother was a Jewish girl from the north and his father a carpenter called Joseph, evidently descended from the royal family of King David. There are a number of rumours about his birth; Joseph and Mary were evidently only engaged and it was said by some that she had become pregnant, not by Joseph, but as the result of a unique spiritual experience. She is said to have described it as a visitation from an angel, a miracle. Quite apart from that, some people claim that the birth itself was surrounded by a number of odd events — voices of angels in the sky and a visit by astrologers from the east — but maybe these were just legends which grew up later.

The child grew up in the small town of Nazareth, north-west of the Lake of Tiberias (called Galilee by the Jews). Nothing much appears to be known about his childhood and youth, although there is a story that he once got left behind after a family visit to Jerusalem and was found talking somewhat precociously with the temple elders.

He came to public attention for the first time when he was about thirty years old. An agitator calling himself John the Baptist was rallying people to his side by the Jordan River when Jesus appeared, asking to be enrolled. Accounts differ as to what actually happened. Some say that the sky opened and a heavenly dove appeared, and some say there was a voice from the sky; it is impossible to be sure. But there is no doubt at all that the event marked the beginning of Jesus' public career.

From then on, it is difficult to sort out the threads in all the confused and sometimes contradictory accounts that have emerged from interviews with the witnesses. It is impossible to put them together into any kind of continuous order. All we can do is to piece them together according to a number of broad themes which describe the events that followed.

One thing seems clear, however. Immediately after his baptism in the Jordan, Jesus left the river and retreated into the desert region to the east. There he is said to have prepared himself for the work he was to do. (His followers say that he had a personal encounter with the devil!) He then returned to the public eye with a preaching tour of the country to the north of Lake Galilee.

One of his first actions was to recruit a team of lieutenants who were to follow him for the next three years, and were eventually to be the leaders of the movement after his death. They seem to have come from a variety of backgrounds, including some of dubious political colour! One, Simon, was certainly a member of the Zealot terrorist organization. What is impressive is that they have apparently given up everything in order to follow him. Even now, after his death, they seem to be, if anything, more dedicated than ever, putting up with violence from the mob and harassment from the authorities.

Jesus continued his work for about three years. Accounts differ as to the course of events and even the places visited during those years. For example, at least one witness (John) says that Jesus visited the capital several times during that period for the religious festivals; yet others (Matthew, Mark, and Luke) claim that he went there for the first time at the end of his life, just before his arrest and downfall.

During those years, it is possible to paint only a series of impressions. He was undoubtedly a very effective healer; wherever he went, the sick were brought to him. Except in his home town, there are no accounts of his having failed to heal anyone. He also claimed to be able to forgive people their sins, which did not make him popular with the Jewish clergy. The Jews consider sin to be the fundamental barrier between man and God; only God has the authority and the power to forgive it. Anyone who claims to be able to forgive people is seen to be abrogating the power of God himself. Yet according to all accounts, this is precisely what Jesus repeatedly did.

Jesus evidently spent a lot of time with his immediate followers. These probably included a number of women as well as the "twelve," who seem to have been of special importance. He is said to have spent many hours with them, sharing his ideas and teaching them about his mission.

What *was* his teaching? And what was the message that he is said to have proclaimed, both to his immediate friends and on the many occasions when he spoke in public? This is not easy to understand if we are not Jews of the first century A.D. It only makes sense in the context of the Jewish ideas and hopes of the time. John the Baptist had already been announcing the impending "kingdom of God," a time when God was expected to take a new initiative in history and deliver His people from their slavery. It was to be a time when the captive would be released, the poor relieved, and peace established. John and his followers hoped all this would be accomplished by the coming of one who would be "anointed" with God's Holy Spirit and — in the power and with the authority of God — would lead the people into this new age as their king.

It seems that Jesus, right from the start, went about and announced that the kingdom was already "breaking in" upon Israel. The miraculous healings and many other amazing things that he did were, he said, signs that this was actually taking place. They had simply to open their eyes and their minds to see and understand. And he seems to have encouraged his followers to believe that he was the expected Messiah, the one who was *even then* anointed and filled with God's Spirit.

Yet his message also seems to have broken out of the intensely nationalistic mould of Jewish expectation. Several times Jesus hinted that this kingdom was not simply for the Jewish people but for others as well. For example, he held out the prospect of eternal life to the non-Jewish woman at the drinking well in Samaria. The term "eternal life" (or "fullness of life") was another phrase that Jesus used interchangeably with the kingdom of God. To be in God's kingdom — or for the kingdom of God to be within you — meant much the same as having "new" or "eternal" life. Whatever these phrases meant, it seems that Jesus was making his offer not only to Jews but to all who had faith in him and were prepared to follow him.

It was this kind of talk, no doubt, that made Jesus so unpopular with the religious leaders and clergy — this and some salty abuse which he is said to have heaped upon them on a number of occasions. Like so many professionally religious people, they had come to believe that they had all the answers, and had become notoriously "holier-than-thou" as a result. Jesus, by all accounts, took delight in pointing out their hypocrisy; so inevitably they began to seek ways of getting rid of him.

By the end of the third year, the opposition to Jesus had evidently built up to such a degree that the Jewish Council in Jerusalem (the council that was responsible to the Roman governor for all Jewish affairs) determined upon his arrest and execution. His ideas had simply become too threatening. No doubt the Roman authorities were also unhappy about having this man and his followers at large. Anyone who led a popular movement which preached possible subversion was a potential danger to the state. Jesus' only supporters seem to have been his immediate followers and the unorganized and politically weak common people.

His end was inevitable, and the accounts of it are in general agreement. One of his recruits, a man named Judas (who probably had strong nationalist sympathies) betrayed him to the Jewish council on the eve of a festival, when Jesus and his followers were in Jerusalem. He was arrested by some soldiers in a thicket on the edge of the city and immediately brought up for trial. The council was anxious to get him tried and out of the way before the coming festival, and before popular support for him could be mustered. Accounts of the court hearings differ somewhat, but he was certainly brought before the Jewish high priest, who found him guilty on a charge of blasphemy. He was then taken before Pilate, the Roman governor, who alone had power to sentence a criminal to death. There is some question about Pilate's attitude at this juncture. Some consider that he believed Jesus innocent of any real crime and so tried to have him released under a local amnesty law. Others think that he was only too happy to concur with the hierarchy's request and to eliminate a potential trouble-maker.

Whatever the truth about his inner feelings, the result was the same. The verdict of the high priest's court was confirmed, and Pilate passed the sentence of death by crucifixion. The sentence was to be carried out immediately so that the whole affair could be tidily cleared up before the religious holiday on Saturday. Jesus was therefore taken to a place of execution outside the city (so as not to profane its sacredness) and executed by a detachment of Roman soldiers. Within three hours, he was certified as dead. His body was taken away by his family and some followers, and immediately placed in a cave-like burial place which had been put at their disposal by a member of the council who was known to have been a private admirer of Jesus. Some say that, because of a threat that the body would be stolen, a guard was set on the tomb by the military.

Nothing happened on the Saturday, the day of the festival, but on the morning of the Sunday it is said that some of his followers went to the tomb and found the body gone. Accounts differ about the precise details, but all agree that the body had disappeared. Following this, it seems that a sizeable number of people saw Jesus alive in a variety of different places. It is impossible to put these appearances into any kind of logical order, but there is no doubt about the sincerity of those who claim to have witnessed these appearances. In fact, they seem willing to face death rather than deny them. Questioned about the sightings, they say that he was not like a ghost or spirit, although he does seem to have materialized and disappeared quite inexplicably. They say that he had on him the marks of his execution, that one of them actually felt the wounds with his own hands, and that the "appearance" ate and drank with them as in the past.

Finally, they say, he disappeared from them and has not been seen since. Again, witnesses differ about the details of this, but they all agree that, after a final talk in which he commanded them to continue his work, he left them, claiming that he was "returning to the Father," by which he clearly meant God. Despite harassment by the Jews and warnings from the Roman authorities, his followers have refused to retract their claims. They insist he is still "living" in some mysterious way.

So might a typical journalist's account of Jesus' life have concluded. It sums up the basic, uninterpreted facts of his career, and would not be disputed by any objective historian. It gives us a glimpse of the man whom his followers came to know during the three dramatic years of his ministry.

B Jesus the Christ

We can only imagine the emotions and questions which must have filled the minds of his followers. Jesus was, to say the least, a strange and awe-inspiring figure. His miracles, his astounding power to heal, and his claims to be able to forgive people, must have deeply disturbed them. Above all, there was the final climax of his reappearance after they had actually seen him dead and buried. How were they to make sense of it all? Who was this man and what had he been doing? Quite clearly, there was more to it than just the superficial events of his life.

Again, they must have reflected on what he had said to them and to the crowds during those three years together. More especially, there was the teaching he had shared during their evenings together as well as their many conversations. What was this "kingdom?" What did he really mean by "eternal life?" What did Jesus mean when he said "born again?" His words were full of mystery, and they puzzled as much as they enlightened. And what about the hints he had given them about who he really was? Not just an anonymous carpenter's son from Nazareth but . . . who? He had never really spelled it out to them, but he had allowed them to guess and had even hinted at the answer. Above all, he had called Peter "blessed" when, one day on the road to Caesarea, he had blurted out: "You are the messiah." What did that mean? Certainly, every Jew had been looking forward to the coming of the messiah who was to save Israel from the Romans. But a messiah who was to suffer and die at their hands . . . what kind of a messiah was that? Certainly not the one they had been expecting.

The minds of his friends must have been buzzing with such questions. Slowly, in the months and years that followed, they began to put the answers together. As Christians, we believe that they were guided in this process by the Holy Spirit, so that the answers they left with us are a true revelation from God. Those answers became the preaching of the early church, and they were ultimately to be expressed in the formal language of the three creeds, which today are in our Book of Common Prayer.

The interpretation which the first Christians put upon those facts may be summarized as follows:

The Theological Interpretation of Who Jesus Was and What He Had Been Doing

Birth   Interpreted as the Incarnation of the Son of God. His ministry thus became a revelation of the nature and purposes of God.

Death   Interpreted as an Atonement achieved between

God and man by his sacrifice on the Cross.

Reappearance   Interpreted as the Resurrection of the Son of God, indicating his victory over the powers of evil and death and the possibility of new life for mankind.

Disappearance   Interpreted as the Ascension of the Son of God. His task accomplished, he returns to the Father.

The person and the work of Jesus may thus be briefly summed up under the four headings: incarnation, atonement, resurrection, and ascension. These give us four perspectives for our understanding of who Jesus really was and what he had been doing.

1   Incarnation

Behind this single word lies the truth of who Jesus truly was and what had taken place in the womb of Mary, his mother. Jesus' followers must have been struck by a difficult paradox. On the one hand, they knew Jesus to have been a man. They had been able to see, touch, hear, and smell him. He ate, drank, got angry, and cried. He was a man; there could be no doubt about that. But he was also someone else. Jesus did things no man had ever done before. He seemed to have a strange intimacy with God, whom he called "Father" in a more intimate way than they did. How could a man possess such extraordinary powers? How could his followers interpret the veiled references to himself in relation to God? And then there was the most shattering event of all: he had come alive again after his certain death. He seemed to be—and had even hinted at being—divine. But how could he possibly be both human and divine? How could his followers express what seemed to be an irreconcilable paradox?

The answer was childishly simple. Jesus was already recognized as the Messiah, the Christ upon whom God's Spirit had been poured out. But his followers now went a step further; they said that he was the Son of God. This was a neat and simple answer, a way of saying that he was *at-one-with* at the same time as being *separate-from* God the Father. In much the same way I can say that, as my father's son, there is much of him in me, yet we are both distinct persons. This was a powerful way of expressing what they believed to be true about Jesus.

The word "incarnation" conveyed the belief that God had actually "taken flesh" (the words literally mean "enfleshed") in the womb of Mary, and that Jesus had been a living embodiment of God during his days on earth. When men had seen and listened to him, they had in a mysterious sense seen and listened to God. John expressed this truth in a tight theological formula by saying that, "The Word (God) became flesh . . . and we beheld Him" (John 1.14). Paul put it another way by saying: "God was in Christ" (2 Cor. 5.19). When we see how the four Gospels of the New Testament were written and put together, we shall see how they were composed not so much as biographies of Jesus the man but very deliberately as *theological* documents designed to interpret and proclaim who Jesus was and what the drama of his life had signified. This process of interpretation naturally continued, and gradually came to be expressed in the formulation of the great creeds of the Catholic Church which tried to define, among other things, who Jesus was. For this reason we repeat in the Eucharist every Sunday these phrases from the Nicene Creed.

> God of God, Light of Light,
> True God of True God,
> Begotten not made,
> Being of one substance with the Father,
> Who, for our sake, came down from heaven
> and was incarnate

2 Atonement

Why had Jesus come among us? The answer, in its simplest form, is that he had come to deal with the problem of human sin. As we saw in the Introduction, "sin" was the word given to all that separates mankind from God. It is the result of a flaw in the human personality, a flaw which inclines every person to turn in upon himself and away from God. As a result, sin destroys the unity or "one-ness" which should ideally exist not only between man and God but also between each man and his neighbour, and each man and his true self. Hence, we see the common situation in which society is divided and in which each individual's wholeness is "dis-integrated" or "dis-eased." We know it is God's will that every one of us should live in unity or harmony with ourselves, with other people, and with him, but there is something about our very humanity that makes this impossible to achieve. A Jew knew this to be true. He was deeply aware of the consequences of sin, both for the individual and for humanity as a whole. He looked to the intervention of God, to the coming of one who would deal with this, who would overcome the power of evil, would deliver people from their sins, and bring in a new order in which God would be in his proper place, at the centre.

When the first Christians came to interpret the work of Jesus, they naturally saw him as the fulfillment of these hopes, now devoid of their nationalistic overtones. He had not delivered Israel from the Roman military force; instead he had delivered mankind from something far more sinister, from the power of evil itself.

How was all this to be expressed? No one image or set of images could do full justice to what Jesus had achieved; so we have in the New Testament and in the interpretations that followed it, a whole series of images. At their root was one central idea: the ultimate purpose and result of the drama of Jesus was the atonement or the *reconciliation*, which was made possible between God and man. And of course, this resulted in the healing ("making whole") between and within men and women. Here are some of the descriptive images used by the New Testament writers.

Jesus was seen as the *victor*, the one who faced and triumphed over the powers of evil. This was evident in his active ministry, when he frequently confronted and cast out demons and evil spirits. Above all, it was shown on the cross, when Jesus allowed the power of evil to do its worst, even allowing himself to be killed. But he demonstrated his victory by breaking the power of death and rising to life again. Through this victory he has made it possible for *us* to overcome, with his strength, the very same powers of evil. This theme of Jesus as victor was symbolically portrayed in the Book of Revelation, which was written largely to show how the crucial battle had been won and the ultimate victory assured.

Jesus was also seen as the *sacrificial victim*. Both Saint Paul and the writer of the Epistle to the Hebrews made use of the images of sacrifice, which were very familiar to the Jews. To put it simply, offering a sacrifice to God had been seen from the most ancient times as a way of "getting on the right side" of God. By offering him a bullock, a lamb, or even a bird or two (which would be ritually killed by the priest in the temple), it was felt that one could turn aside God's anger; he would be "satisfied" and therefore willing to release his people from punishment. Even though this idea had been frequently challenged by some of the prophets as being naive and simply untrue, it was something deeply ingrained in the Hebrew mind. Even the most optimistic Jew realized that all the animal sacrifices in the world would do no more than keep God happy for a short time.

Here, then, was a way of interpreting the work and achievement of Jesus. The early Christians simply described Jesus and his death on the cross as the "one perfect sacrifice," so complete that it rendered all other sacrifices redundant. In Jesus, God had sacrificed his own life and this had effectively succeeded where all else had failed. Jesus came to be described as the sacrificial "Lamb of God," who had poured out his own blood. It is no coincidence that John describes the death of Jesus just at the time the lambs were being killed in the temple for the coming festival. The writer to the Hebrews portrays Jesus as the only true High Priest who has offered his own life as the perfect sacrifice (Hebrews 4.12–5.10).

A sacrifice was traditionally meant to satisfy God; John talks of Jesus' death as being an *"expiation"* and a *"propitiation"* for human sin (1 John 2.12). The image should not be, and was not meant to be, pushed too far, as if a loving Jesus has to propitiate an angry and wrathful Father. It is meant to show how sin must somehow be paid for and how, in dying on the cross, Jesus paid for it with his life.

This led Saint Paul to talk of Jesus paying the "ransom" price in order to "redeem" people from their slavery to sin. In his day, when a great number of the population were slaves, one way of escaping from bondage was to pay a redemption price to one's owner. One could then be released from slavery and become a free man. Probably all of the early Christians had experienced their conversion to Jesus as a "freeing," above all a freedom from sin and its consequences; so the image of redemption was one which would have been readily understood.

Jesus as *Saviour or deliverer* also made a great deal of sense to

the first Jewish Christians. For decades, these Jews had antici-
pated God's intervention through history to deliver Israel from
her oppressors. They had looked for the coming of the new
kingdom in which the prisoners would be set free and the poor
and oppressed would be saved. Jesus had *not* ushered in a new
Jewish state, but the first Christians believed that he *had* inaugurated a new order. And within this new order they experienced
salvation and *liberation*, not from the outward power of the
Roman army, but from the inward powers of sin, evil, and
disease. Jesus was seen as the bearer of salvation from sin and as
the healer and absolver. "Who is there to rescue me out of this
body doomed to death?" asked Paul. He proceeded to answer his
own question: "God alone, through Jesus Christ our Lord!"
(Romans 7.24–25).

These were some of the images used to describe the work of
Jesus. But underlying them all was the fundamental conviction
that he had made possible a totally new relationship between
God and man; as a result of what Jesus had done, man could now
be at-one with God.

3 Resurrection

In the light of all these expectations, the reappearance of Jesus
on the third day was interpreted as the actual resurrection of the
Son of God from the dead. Jesus had paid the price and achieved
the victory in his death on the cross. In his reappearance, that
victory was proclaimed and demonstrated. As Peter told the
people in Jerusalem not long afterward, the man they had killed
was alive: "He has been raised by God, as we can all bear
witness" (Acts 2.32). There was no doubt about it. The proof
had been there to see. The meaning of that strange coming-
alive-again was that God had raised up his Son for all to see.
Historically, it was the living proof that Jesus was more than a
mere man; theologically, it expressed the faith of the early
Christians that God's work in Jesus had been crowned with suc-
cess. It was a sign that all who followed Jesus might similarly be
"resurrected" to eternal life.

4 Ascension

The final disappearance of Jesus was the last act of his visible,
earthly ministry among his followers. It soon came to be interpreted as his ascension into heaven. It is interesting that,

according to the critics, the earliest version of the story in Saint Luke's Gospel simply says that Jesus "parted from them" (Luke 24.51). Only at a later stage were the words added about being carried up into heaven. The addition of the latter phrase was meant to underline the idea not of disappearance (from physical view) but ascension (into heaven). In fact, the idea of an ascension suitably rounded off the story of the descent of the pre-existent Son of God to earth. The Son had "come down" and been born to the Virgin Mary. He had died and "descended" further into the depths of hell (as the creeds later expressed it), and then "risen up" to earth again. Finally, to complete the drama, the divine Son returns. He ascends to heaven again and is restored to his place at the Father's right hand.

A Biblical View of the Universe

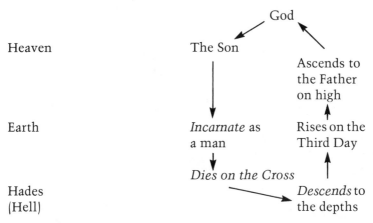

It is important to recognize that this is not the language of history; it is an attempt to give expression or "form" to the conviction of the first Christians that what Jesus had done was cosmic in its significance, and affected all men across the boundaries of time and space. Christ's life could never be fully explained. Have we, two thousand years later, thought of a better way to describe this mystery?

Many years later, the church evolved the liturgical year upon which its annual cycle of worship and observances was based. As we shall see later, this liturgical year was based soundly upon these great beliefs of the faith together with the belief in the gift of the Holy Spirit at Pentecost (see Chapter 8), which forms the final great event of the Christian drama. The diagram below shows how, beginning with the basic historical events of Jesus' life, the Christian church added its interpretation and ultimately came to express these events in its annual cycle of worship.

Historical Event	Theological Key Word	What It Means	Liturgical Season
1 Birth	Incarnation	Tells us *who* Jesus is.	Christmas
2 Death	Atonement	Tells us *what* he accomplished.	Good Friday
Reappearance	Resurrection	Demonstration and proof of his victory. Sign of the new life being stronger than death.	Easter
3 Disappearance	Ascension	Completion of his work.	Ascension Day

7

How the New Testament Was Written

The last chapter told us something of the historical life of Jesus, insofar as it is possible to reconstruct it, and explained how the first Christians interpreted these amazing events. It is time now to pause and look at the actual records that are available, the books of the New Testament, without which we would have hardly any evidence at all of Jesus and the early church.

Some people regard the New Testament as the literal word of God — each word is believed to be directly inspired by God and, therefore, literally true. According to this view (called "fundamentalism"), every single event took place precisely as it is recorded, and every word was said exactly as it is written down. Although the early thinkers and theologians of the church were not under this impression (and, indeed, went to considerable lengths to interpret the sometimes contradictory texts of the Bible), people increasingly came to treat the text in this rigid manner. However, over about the last hundred years, the science of biblical criticism has been developed, and this has led to a much more sophisticated knowledge of how the Bible was put together. There are three types of biblical criticism, reflecting the three stages of its development as a science over the last century.

1 **Textual Criticism** arose when it became apparent that, in the process of the New Testament's translation and copying, a wide variety of "texts" had emerged. This development should not surprise anyone, considering what happens when books are translated and passed down over centuries. The original language of Jesus and his followers was Aramaic, a dialect of

Hebrew. In order to get their message across to their early readers, the writers of the New Testament had to translate all of this into Greek, the common language at that time. Centuries later, it had to be translated again into Latin and, later still, into vernacular languages such as German, English, and French.

As well as linguistic changes to the text, mistakes inevitably occurred while the books were being copied from generation to generation. We must remember that printing was not invented until 1500 years after Christ. The early scribes and monks had to painstakingly copy these documents by hand, and of course all kinds of errors must have crept in. As each erroneous copy was copied, the errors were repeated and compounded over many generations.

A hundred years ago, scholars recognized this problem, and so the science of textual criticism was developed in an attempt to get back to the earliest and purest texts. The actual documents were, of course, long ago decayed, but by a complicated system of analysis and comparison of existing texts, it was possible to discover "family trees" of texts pointing back in time to their originals. In this way, critics were able to reconstruct not a perfect text (it is probably impossible to know exactly), but at least one which is as genuine as possible. It is upon such reconstructed texts that our modern translations are based.

2   Source Criticism. While these scholars were busy at their work of comparing ancient texts, it became obvious to them that the documents of the Gospels which we now have are not, in themselves, the *original* sources of the stories, events, and sayings they record. Rather, they point back to other, earlier sources which the writers used in constructing their Gospels. The most obvious clue to these sources is the fact that slightly different versions of the same event or saying appear in the same Gospel.[16] Moreover, we often find very similar descriptions being given by two or even three writers.[17] Once such clues had been recognized, these critics began to look at the Gospels in a different fashion. It rapidly became obvious that the evangelists were compilers, editors, and commentators, rather than eye-witnesses or recorders of the events they described. It became clear that they were assembling material which had already been collected in either written or spoken form.

As a result, scholars began to use their skills to see if they could discover the sources which pre-dated the Gospels. In doing so, they were getting closer to the actual eye-witness accounts and thus to the events and the sayings themselves. This process was also applied to the other books of the New Testament, in an attempt to get behind the forms in which they have eventually come down to us.

3   Form Criticism. This is a more recent development in New Testament criticism, and it arose as scholars attempted to push back farther, beyond the original written stories of the Gospels. Having reconstructed, for example, a source document called "X," let us imagine that it contained a series of parables. Inevitably we are led to ask: "How authentic are they? How close are they to the actual words of Jesus?" Here the form critics go to work. They began by recognizing that each parable had in fact been passed on from the original witnesses, through a whole line of people, until it reached its final "form" in the written collection. The crucial step was now this: in the process of such oral transmission, it is possible to detect certain influences at work, all of which leave their mark on the final shape of the parable. By detecting the effects of these influences upon each parable, it is possible to work backward and get some idea of the original form of the parable. This applies not only to the parables, of course, but more or less equally to all the literary forms we find in the Gospels. Over the years, considerable studies have been made of them all.[18]

The combined effects of textual, source, and form criticism have transformed our understanding of the New Testament and taken us beyond the existing texts, far closer to the events and sayings that they record. It has naturally shed new light on these contents and enriched our understanding of Jesus and his message. Nearly all modern commentaries on the New Testament have benefitted from the fruits of this kind of research.

What Is In The New Testament?

The New Testament is made up of four different kinds of books.
1 The four Gospels, telling of events and sayings in the life of Jesus.
2 A collection of narratives from the life of the early church,

chiefly to do with Peter and Paul, called the Acts of the Apostles.

3 A series of letters (epistles) written by early Christian leaders.
4 The final book, Revelation, a series of letters in the traditional Jewish style of "apocalyptic."

For approximately three centuries after this material came into existence, it was not bound together in any one book. It formed part of a much larger and ever-growing volume of letters, Gospels, and teachings which circulated among the members of the early churches. However, a process of sorting gradually took place, and the books of the New Testament came to be recognized by all the churches as having a special authority, in fact, the authority of the original apostles. Literally speaking, this was wrong; the New Testament was not actually written by the apostles. But the churches were correct in their basic assumption: the New Testament does express the faith and teaching of those original apostles. And for this reason it has authority for us today.

1   The Gospels

Scholars usually begin by separating the first three Gospels from the last. Saint John's Gospel, it is generally agreed, was written considerably later than the others and does not seem to have any direct connection with them. In contrast, the other three all "hang together" and are therefore called the synoptic Gospels (this is what the Greek word *synoptic* means). There are several theories to account for their origin; what follows is one of these generally-accepted theories.

The original witnesses of Jesus' life and sayings kept their reminiscences to their own circle. But after his Ascension, they were passed on by word of mouth through the growing Christian communities in ever-widening circles, being embellished and streamlined in the process. Each local or regional church began to build up its own collection. Central to all these collections were the all-important details of Jesus' last days: his arrest, trial, execution, burial, and resurrection. These events lay at the core of their faith. In addition, the churches remembered the miraculous events, healings, parables, teachings, confrontations, and controversies. All of these memories would have been treasured and eventually written down, so that the major

Christian communities would certainly have compiled their own written collections. It is these that were probably the sources used by the writers of the first three Gospels. There may also have been other, more personal sources of information contributed by original witnesses, for example, but most of the material in the Gospels would have come from the written collections. Here, in diagram form, is one illustration of the development that might have taken place.[19]

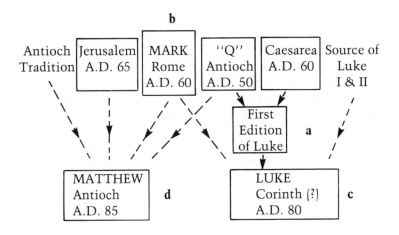

a   The very first compilation may well have been an earlier edition of the present Gospel of Saint Luke, with material from a source called "Q" (*Quelle*, the German word for source), which contained many of the parables.

b   At about the same time as Luke was putting together his first edition, Saint Mark was busy writing up the tradition of the Christian community in Rome. The material in this Roman collection may well have been supplemented and given special authority by the fact that Peter himself was almost certainly a member of that team; so many of the events in Mark's Gospel are possibly eyewitness accounts.

c   Sometime before A.D. 80, Luke found Mark's Gospel and

proceeded to incorporate it into a new edition of his own. At the beginning he added some other accounts of Jesus not included by Mark. This final version was probably written when Luke was in Corinth.

d   Some time after these two evangelists were writing, Matthew assembled his Gospel with another audience in mind. He almost certainly had a copy of Mark's Gospel with him when he wrote, because he seems to have taken Mark's structure and material and added material from other sources. It has been suggested that his unique source was the mother church in Jerusalem itself, and that Matthew was writing with a predominantly Jewish background.

These three writers made use of all the material they had at hand, forming it into our first three Gospels. Each one was designed not only to record the events, but more significantly, to proclaim the truth about Jesus and to convert people to faith in him.

The case of the fourth Gospel is somewhat different, although this difference must not be exaggerated. Like the other Gospels, it is based on a particular tradition (or collection of traditions) about Jesus, collected and compiled by a later writer. In this case the traditions were probably those of the church at Ephesus. It was reputed that the Apostle John had finally gone to live in the region of Ephesus. This would give credence to the belief that he had written the Gospel, and would also give it a special authority. Whether or not this link is true, it is certain that there was another John who was called the Seer of Patmos (an island near Ephesus) whose successor (yet another John) probably wrote the Gospel based on the traditions of that community.

The style of the fourth Gospel is quite different from that of the other three. It was written later, when there had been time to ponder the meaning of the events in Jesus' life. Consequently, it has been labelled a theological rather than a strictly historical work. This description is partly accurate — John's Gospel is certainly a profoundly theological text — but there has been an increasing recognition that the other three are theological as well. The theological nature of Saint John's Gospel was simply more obvious.

In the Gospels, then, we have four different accounts of the life and teaching of Jesus which provide us with nearly all our information about him.

2 The Acts of the Apostles

This book is in fact a continuation of the third Gospel, and it almost certainly comes from the hand of the same author. The first few verses make it quite clear that, in its final form at least, Acts was written by Luke; there is no doubt that its first chapter is intended to follow on from the last chapter in Luke's Gospel. (Compare the opening verses of Luke and Acts, and it immediately becomes obvious that the two are intended to be taken together.) Acts purports to tell the story, albeit somewhat sketchily, of the early days of the church's life. It begins with a series of vignettes, moves to an account of some of Saint Peter's experiences, and then develops into a continuous narrative of Saint Paul's travels as a missionary. However, Acts is not strictly a narrative. Like the Gospels, it is a kind of propaganda document. Peter's speech in Acts 2.14 ff., for example, is not simply a verbatim report of a particular speech that Peter made on a particular occasion. Rather, it is a typical model of the kind of message that was proclaimed by Peter and the early Christians and which Luke himself was anxious to convey. The same could probably be said of the contents of Saint Stephen's speech (Acts 7), although we cannot deny several points: Stephen *did* speak; his speech marked a breaking point in Jewish-Christian relations; he was stoned to death as a consequence; and Saul was partly responsible. What we have in Acts is a solid basis of historical facts, worked into a very forceful story by its author, in an attempt to illustrate the amazing expansion of that first small group of disciples to form the Holy Catholic Church.

3 The Epistles

The nature of the epistles needs little explanation. They are just what they claim to be — letters written by early Christian leaders and circulated among the first Christian communities. But there is some uncertainty about who wrote them, when they were written, and to whom. It is reasonably certain, for example, that Saint Paul did not write all the letters personally attributed to him. The radical differences in literary style are obvious. In addition, the situations reflected in some of the epistles clearly occurred later than his death. The same can be said of those writings attributed to Saint Peter. For example, the kind of persecution reflected in 1 Peter does not appear to have occurred until the beginning of the second century, long after Peter's death. Why the names of these venerated apostles were attached to these somewhat later letters is unknown, but the practice was commonly accepted at the time. It was thought quite normal for an author to put another, more famous name to his work in order to give it authority and attract more readers. It would not have been thought wrong, in other words, for a later Christian author to have issued a letter in the name of Peter or Paul if he sincerely thought he was being true to their teaching. Thus scholars are doubtful about the true authorship and date of some epistles, but this does not diminish their value.

In such a brief survey, it is impossible to go into the contents or detail of all the epistles, but here is a simplified table of those attributed to Saint Paul.[20]

Group a

Galatians	written from Syrian Antioch	A.D. 48
1 Thessalonians	written from Corinth	A.D. 50
2 Thessalonians	written from Corinth	A.D. 50

Group b

1 Corinthians	written from Ephesus	A.D. 54
Philippians	written from Ephesus	A.D. 54 (?)
2 Corinthians chapters 10–13	written from Ephesus	A.D. 55
2 Corinthians chapters 1–9	written from Macedonia	A.D. 55/56
Romans	written from Corinth	A.D. 57

Group c (Written during Paul's captivity)

Colossians	written from Rome	A.D. 60/61 (?)
Philemon	written from Rome	A.D. 60/61 (?)
Ephesians	written from Rome	A.D. 60/61 (?)

Group d (Attributed to, but probably not written by, Paul)

Titus	written from Ephesus	after A.D. 62
1Timothy	written from Macedonia	after A.D. 62
2 Timothy	written from Rome	after A.D. 62

In addition to these Pauline epistles, there are several others written in varying circumstances. The substance of *Hebrews* is not Pauline, despite its claim, and its form is more that of a sermon, despite its ending. It was probably the work of a Greek-speaking convert of the second century, writing to a group of Christians. Like the author, they had roots in the Jewish past; Jesus would best be understood as the fulfillment of their Hebrew tradition.

Another group of seven letters has been referred to as the "catholic epistles" (that is, "orthodox") since the beginning of the fourth century. They were distinguished in this way, not from the other New Testament epistles, but from a number of others in circulation at the time which were far from orthodox in their teachings. They differ from the rest of the New Testament epistles in that they were not sent to any particular Christian community but are all "general" epistles written to the church at large. Here are these seven epistles:

James — Scholars are undecided about the identity of this particular James. The epistle was written very early in the church's life to a group of Jewish Christians, probably living in Palestine. The ideas reflect the practical struggles of the young church trying to live up to the radical demands of Jesus.

1 Peter — Scholars vary in their estimation of the authority and date of this epistle. If it is indeed by Peter, it is obviously early (A.D. 62), and probably relates to the opposition the Christians were receiving in Galatia. If it is not by Peter, then it is likely dated fifty years later, and refers to persecution taking place in Bithynia, a province in Asia Minor. Some writers suggest that the letter, in essence, has a liturgical origin and grew out of what was once a baptismal address.

2 Peter — This is probably not by the author of 1 Peter and certainly not written by Saint Peter. It is generally regarded as the latest book in the New Testament, possibly written as late as A.D. 140. The purpose of the letter is to correct the readers from false teaching, which is known to have threatened the church in the middle of the second century.

1, 2, and 3 John — The weight of the evidence suggests that all three texts were written by the author of the fourth Gospel. The latter two are simply letters, dealing with particular pastoral problems. The first is a far richer work, and may be read as an extension of the kind of teaching typical of the fourth Gospel.

Jude — This is possibly written by Jude, the "brother of the Lord." It was most likely written in Palestine and intended for a small church (or group of churches) for whom the author had a sense of pastoral responsibility. It deals with a local emergency — the arrival of false teachers who were perverting the faith.

These notes are, of course, no more than brief descriptions. Readers who wish to go more deeply into questions of authorship and dating, as well as the content and teaching of these fascinating works, should study the Bible with the help of a commentary, some of which I have listed in the bibliography.

4   The Book of Revelation

A commentary is even more essential when readers consider this last work in the New Testament. The Book of Revelation is not easy to understand today, because it belongs to a type of literature with which we are almost entirely unfamiliar. We therefore tend to approach it as either a piece of historical forecasting or a web of colourful fantasy, and we succeed only in getting hopelessly confused. But in fact, it belongs largely to a type of writing called "apocalyptic." The word literally means "breaking in upon," and the common theme in nearly all such writing is the breaking in of God upon history, usually in a catastrophic way. Apocalyptic writing appears in the Old Testament in the Book of Daniel, probably written in its final form in the second century B.C., and it occurs again in the slightly later Book of Enoch. The scene is consistently that of God's dramatic intervention in history, accompanied by striking physical events in the skies and on the earth. There is usually some kind of dividing of those who are to be saved and those destined for destruction. Always there is the fundamental struggle between the forces of good and evil, symbolized in such images as angels, dragons, and other mythical beasts. The authors were, in fact, writing about the great cosmic drama they saw taking place (or about to take place) both in and behind history. Through the vivid symbols and images found in dreams and mythology, they conveyed the course of the drama. In the Jewish tradition, all this was seen as taking place through, and partly because of, historical events in the ordinary physical world.

The Book of Revelation comes to us out of this milieu. The author is concerned with what is going on in the life of the particular church communities to whom he writes, for he writes with passionate authority, sternly reproving them for failing to meet God's demands. But he does this against a vivid apocalyptic background, piercing ordinary human events with religious and cosmic significance.

Whether or not the author is John the Evangelist, or perhaps another John called "the Prophet," is still debated by scholars. It is a difficult book to understand, but the use of a good commentary will be richly rewarded.

8

A New Power

In Chapter 6, we depicted the life of Jesus and traced the interpretation put upon it by his first disciples. That story ended
with Jesus' final disappearance from the earth, a disappearance
which marked the conclusion of his earthly ministry. When the
disciples came to give a meaning to that disappearance, they
interpreted it as his ascension, the final stage in the drama
which had begun with the incarnation and reached its climax in
the resurrection. The work was now done, and the divine Son,
having inaugurated his kingdom on earth, had returned to ''sit
at God's right hand.'' The drama appears to be over, with the
ends neatly tied. All that is left for us to do is to proclaim the
good news of Jesus' victory and follow him in our own day and
age.

This is often preached as the Christian Gospel: ''Jesus is Lord!
Follow him!'' But this is *not* the end of the story; nor indeed is it
the whole of the Gospel. There is more to be told.

If we go back to the end of Saint Luke's Gospel (Luke 24.45
ff.), the risen Christ is talking to his followers prior to his final
departure. He is commissioning them to carry on his work and
to proclaim the good news ''to all nations, beginning in
Jerusalem.'' Having given them their marching orders,
however, he issues an abrupt command: ''But don't go yet. Wait
here in the city until the power from above comes down upon
you.'' They need the power necessary to go out and do their
work. Despite the good news of Jesus' resurrection, they are still
just ordinary men and women, very human and very weak.
Only when they have received power from God will they be able
to go and live the kind of lives which God desires. Until then
they are as useless as a dishwasher or a light bulb without elec-
tric power.

But how were they to receive this power? Jesus had already
given them some clues, if we are to believe his many sayings in

John's Gospel. He had promised that the same Holy Spirit, which had in the past fallen upon the prophets and appeared at his baptism, would shortly fall upon them and fill them with his power.

It is worth pausing for a moment to reflect on the words *Holy Spirit*. The idea of God's Spirit goes back far into the Jew's understanding of God. The Spirit, in the beginning, was God in his work of infusing life into his creation, animating and enlivening all that he was making. But there is another understanding of these words. Through the Holy Spirit, God empowered certain men and women with special gifts of insight and leadership. Great leaders such as Gideon or Samson (Judges 6 and 14) began their careers as the Spirit of God was "poured out" upon them. Again, it was through the inspiration and power of the Spirit that the great prophets spoke, and they were listened to because other people recognized that God was working through them. It was hoped that one day God would pour out his Spirit on all men (Joel 2.28), so that they would all be able to live in the strength and under the guidance of God. This was an old promise that was part of the Jewish tradition.

And then had come Jesus, a person who was clearly filled with the Spirit of God. When people saw or heard Jesus, they believed he was inspired by God. But he also told his followers how they too would experience the outpouring of God's Spirit in their lives. He promised, in other words, that they would not just be left to follow his example; they would actually be empowered with his divine power. He said they would receive the gift of the Holy Spirit, and God, through his Spirit, would live in them (see especially in John 14).

According to Saint Luke's account, Jesus repeated this promise in the last few moments before he finally left his disciples. He told them to wait in Jerusalem until they had been empowered from on high. And according to the continuation of the story in the Acts of the Apostles, this is precisely what they did. They waited as Jesus had commanded, and one day when they were all together, they suddenly had a most amazing experience. The second chapter of Acts, which depicts this experience, is not a passage to take lightly. Some scholars, unable to accept the reality of such an experience, have attempted to explain it symbolically. They have said, for example, that it is a colourful way of describing what undeniably took place in the space of a very few years — namely, that the early Christians were "on fire" with enthusiasm and took the good news to people speaking all kinds of languages throughout the Roman Empire. But the more recent experiences of many Christians as a result of the charismatic movement in the church have led to a much more literal interpretation of this story of Pentecost. The author of Acts was in fact describing the fulfillment of Jesus' promise; he tells of the empowerment of the first Christians by the Holy Spirit and of the signs that followed. As a result of that dramatic experience, the disciples then went out to convert the world. According to the accounts of their work in Acts and the epistles, they were accompanied by all the signs of the Spirit's activity.

Evidence of this new power was first and most dramatically seen in the phenomenon of "speaking in tongues" which, according to Acts 2, accompanied the outpouring of the Holy Spirit. As a result of their new spiritual power, those Aramaic- and possibly Greek-speaking disciples now began to speak in an amazing variety of languages other than their own. Visitors from all parts of the Empire heard and understood them "in their own tongues." This and the similar phenomenon of "praying in tongues" (not necessarily in any known language) became a common occurrence in early Christian gatherings. But what is more important, the new power led to a boldness and confidence which overcame the initial fear and reticence of the first followers. Pentecost, in the book of Acts, is followed directly by the account of Peter standing up to the hostile Jewish crowd and proclaiming the resurrection of Jesus. The power of the Spirit led directly to the proclamation of the Word. But as Jesus himself had promised, there were also "signs following" (Mark 16.17). Acts tells us of the power of the Holy Spirit in overcoming evil and disease (Acts 5.12 ff., 19.12 ff.). Peter raises the cripple near the entrance to the temple (Acts 3.6), and Paul, after being bitten by a poisonous snake, comes to no harm (Acts 28.14). Clearly a new power was abroad in the world, or to be more precise, within the new Christian community. They called it the gift of the Holy Spirit.

The gift was given to the first church at Pentecost, but how was it given to those who joined the church after that particular event? The answer, quite simply, was that it was given by baptism (as we saw in Chapter 2). It is important to notice its occurrence in this rapid, early development of the church. Baptism was the means by which one became a Christian and so entered this new community; in baptism, one also received the gift of the Holy Spirit and began to lead a renewed life.

How the Early Christians Came to Understand This Experience: The Holy Trinity and the Church

Just as the early Christians had experienced the drama of Jesus' life and then set about interpreting it (thereby giving us the fundamental words of our Christian theology — *incarnation, atonement, resurrection, ascension* — so they also set about interpreting this experience of renewal, which had so profoundly changed their lives. In this way they came to formulate the doctrine of the Holy Trinity and to develop a theology of the church.

1 The Holy Trinity

The experience of Pentecost led to another development in our understanding of God. To the Jews, there was only one God. This was the insight of Isaiah, and it is a basic belief of Judaism (and Islam). It is also a fundamental belief of Christians. The Jews had traditionally called this God by the name "Father," which was also the name that Jesus used in his prayers. Christians, however, have also come to know this one God in another form or person, the human form which the disciples encountered in the person of Jesus. When they called him "Son," they were trying to express the mysterious truth that he was both man and God, yet *not* the same form or person of God which they had hitherto worshipped as Father. (The Latin word *persona* means a mask or appearance.) They therefore expressed this by saying that they worshipped the *one God* whom they had come to know as two persons, *Father* and *Son*.

With the pouring out of the *Spirit* at Pentecost, however, this simple twofold explanation seemed not enough. The first way of describing the mystery was therefore carried a step further. And the one God was said to be three persons united in their "substance" and yet distinct in our experience. He was at the same time:

The Father   —the Creator, whom the Jewish people had worshipped for at least 2,000 years and who was known to all men as God;

The Son   —that *persona* whom men had seen and encountered for roughly thirty years in Palestine, who had existed in the Godhead from before time and had thereafter returned to sit "at the right hand of the Father" (inasmuch as we can picture this in terms of space);

and

The Holy Spirit —that *persona* who is alive now in the church and within each Christian, as God's living presence in us.

This mystery, which is the heart of what Christians believe about God, is called the *Holy Trinity*, and is commonly expressed in the form of a triangle.

Three Persons

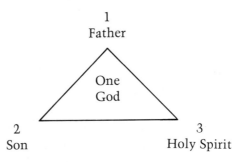

The doctrine of the Holy Trinity is simple as long as we recognize that it is meant to be a picture (or model) of what God is like, based upon the experiences we have had of him. To understand why it is fundamental to Christianity, we have only to deny one of its three assertions:

Deny the Father   — and we really have no God at all;

Deny the Son   — and Jesus becomes merely a man, a
pathetic even if noble example of the
world's supreme idealist;

Deny the Holy Spirit — and we deny that God is alive and
powerful in his followers today. Jesus
remains as a supreme example, but we
have no power to follow him or to overcome sin in our own lives.

2   The Doctrine of the Church

Even while the New Testament was being written, the basic
doctrine of the Holy Trinity was being formulated. For example,
we find it stated quite clearly in Saint Paul's words, which we
now use as a prayer called The Grace: "The grace of Our Lord
Jesus Christ and the love of God (Father) and the fellowship of
the Holy Spirit . . ." (2 Corinthians 13.14). Although it was not
more precisely spelled out in the New Testament, this doctrine
is quite clearly fundamental to the faith of the early Christians
and later formed the framework of the great Christian creeds.

During this early period, Paul in particular reflected upon the
phenomenon of the church and gave us images or models which
have helped us to understand the nature of this new
"organism." A preliminary word is in order here because we
sometimes take the church so much for granted today. Many of
us have become so used to thinking of it solely in terms of a kind
of service club, that we all too easily fail to see how there is
anything unique about the Christian church at all. And yet
there is — and it is something awesome.

Let us go back to the experience of Paul. Paul must have
realized soon after his conversion (described in Acts 9) that he
had found something strange and exciting — and I am talking
not just of his own experience as an individual on the Damascus
Road, but of the corporate experience of the new community he
had entered. When we read his letters in Greek, we are struck by
the frequency of the word *koinonia*, which translates into the
Latin word *communio*. When we translate it into English, the
equivalent word *fellowship* totally fails to convey the rich
meaning behind it. Yet it was a key word used by Paul to express
his experience of new life, for this was in essence a *corporate*

life, a sharing-with-others in the life of God. To Paul it would be totally inconceivable to think of a solitary Christian; the two words were contradictory. Being a Christian actually meant that one had been rescued out of alienation and aloneness, and included as part of a new creation, the church of God.

This church we might best describe as an *organism*, something living and growing, except its life was not simply an ordinary life, but the Holy Spirit of God. Paul tried to express this in his writings, and he came up with a number of images. The most powerful one is that of the Body of Christ. The line of thought is very clear. For roughly thirty years, Paul might have said, God expressed himself through the *physical* body of Jesus of Nazareth, and in that physical body he began his great work of salvation. But that particular body had done its job, and had become the glorified body of the risen and ascended Christ. Since then he has chosen to work through another body, the *"mystical"* body of the church. So it was that Paul said: "Now we are the Body of Christ . . ." (1 Corinthians 12.17), and he went on to describe each one of us as its members, in the sense that hands and feet are members of a human body. As members of this mystical body, we share in its unique life (the Holy Spirit), and we are nourished. As members who are each filled with the Spirit, we each receive gifts which enable us to serve not only one another but also the world. The calling of the Christian, after all, is to carry on Christ's work. Paul went on to say how vital it is that all members realize the importance of their life *in common*. If one suffers, all suffer; if one rejoices, all rejoice; all must care for each other.

> For Christ is like a single body with its many limbs and organs, which, many as they are, together make up one body. For indeed we are all brought into one body by baptism, in the one Spirit . . . and that one Holy Spirit was poured out for us all to drink . . . all its organs (must) feel the same concern for one another. If one organ suffers, they all suffer together. If one flourishes, they all rejoice together. (1 Corinthians 12.12–13 & 26).

In the Acts of the Apostles (2.42 ff.), we read how far this common sharing was carried when Christians sold their goods and possessed everything in common. This is certainly very far from the individualism of our own age! This theology of the church as the Body of Christ has been powerfully revived over the last few decades.

Saint Paul also used other images to describe his experience of the church. He talks of it as the "temple of the Holy Spirit" (1 Corinthians 3.16, 2 Corinthians 6.16, and Ephesians 2.21). The temple, of course, was pre-eminently the place where the Jews thought God was specially present. Peter also spoke of the church as being a "royal priesthood" (1 Peter 2.5,9), expressing the idea that, as members of the church, all Christians shared in the priestly calling of Christ. The "priesthood" of the ordinary Christian calls upon us all to mediate God to our fellow men and to give up, or sacrifice, our lives in his service. To share in Christ's priesthood is thus no easy calling. But it is the image of the church as the Body of Christ that has had the greatest influence on our understanding of *koinonia*, the fellowship we join at our baptism.

9

The Story of the Church

For too many people, the story of Christianity is something that ends abruptly with the close of the New Testament, and resumes again within the last few decades, the span of our living memories. Between the two periods is a great emptiness, filled with a handful of disconnected scraps of history. Protestants may recollect that there was a Reformation three or four hundred years ago; travellers in Europe may have had their imagination stirred by the great cathedrals and the glorious monuments of the mediaeval church; North Americans may remember something of the traditions about the itinerant preachers who travelled about in the days when the West was really wild; and most of us have read something about the missionary exploits of the nineteenth century. But that is often the limit to our knowledge. Few of us have any idea of the rich and fascinating story of the people of God from the time of Pentecost until the present day. Yet for any real understanding of the church in today's world, we need to know something of that story.

In the next two chapters we shall look at the broad trends of these two thousand years of church history, stopping at several points to illustrate some of the more important and interesting facets in greater depth. (I make no secret of the fact that my selection of events and developments is inevitably highly subjective. Also I write from an Anglican bias for which, again, I have no apology!)

A The Early Years: from Christ until c.312 A.D.

The story of the early church grows directly out of the pages of the New Testament, just as in another sense the New Testament itself was a product of that early church. As we read the books of the New Testament, we are able to form a picture of the original Christian communities that first produced and then treasured them. We have a picture of a young, almost explosive group of men and women who, in the space of a very few years, had taken the message of Jesus to practically all parts of the Roman Empire and had succeeded in planting communities of Christians in nearly all the major cities. The marks of this early church were its sheer energy and its rapid expansion. What had begun as a small Jewish sect had become a major new religious movement within just a few decades. It had burst out of its Jewish shell to make converts from the lowest to the highest levels of Roman society. The signal for this rapid expansion seems to have been the preaching of Stephen (Acts 8.1,4), a Greek-speaking Christian who first planted the seeds of the idea that the Gospel was not only for Jews but for *all* men and women.

Saint Peter struggled with this idea, as we gather from the evidence in Acts (Chapter 10),[21] but he finally admitted the universality of the Gospel. Paul took a step further, and the Acts of the Apostles tells of the rapid spread of the faith from Palestine to many parts of the central and eastern Empire. Here the news of the Gospel was greeted with growing enthusiasm by non-Jews, who were eventually to outnumber by far the original Jewish believers. All over the Empire, these new Christian communities grew up, beginning in the cities and slowly spreading into the countryside.

What were these first simple communities like? We find pictures of them in the epistles. The first letter to the Corinthians gives us a particularly vivid account. The Christians in Corinth were much more turbulent and free-wheeling than our average congregation today — the evidence of the Holy Spirit was readily apparent. The obvious gifts of the Holy Spirit (1 Corinthians 12) were frequently counterbalanced by personality clashes which at one time threatened to tear the community apart (1 Corinthians 1.10 ff.). There was clearly a leadership struggle. Rival factions split the unity by following different leaders. Paul had to admonish the people and tell them how their gifts should be used for the building up of the "Body." He was led to the classic conclusion that the chief mark of the Spirit is the quality of love (*agape* in Greek), which the Spirit creates and which binds the members into one (1 Corinthians 13).

Some kind of governmental structure was clearly needed and it very rapidly came into being. Unfortunately it is not possible to see it fully developed within the New Testament era, but by the time the church emerged from the "tunnel period" (approx. A.D. 70–110), it had developed the threefold system which has continued within Catholic Christianity until the present.

We do not know with any precision who founded all the first Christian communities. Saint Paul was undoubtedly responsible for some, although even in his case others had frequently been there before him. In each of the new communities, a leader was appointed. The actual method of appointment remains unspecified, although we do know that Paul named leaders (and commissioned them by the laying-on of hands) who were to act as overseers of each local church. The clearest reference to this is in 2 Timothy 1.6–7. The letter is written to Timothy, the *episcopos* of a church, and the reference is clearly to an act of ordination or setting apart which Timothy had received through the laying-on of hands. It would seem that this was almost certainly the means by which leaders were commissioned and empowered for their work. There is little doubt that such setting apart would have been understood as a conferring of apostolic authority on the leaders.

These leaders of the early Christian communities were called *episcopoi* or bishops; their function was to exercise Christian authority over their communities, preside at the sacraments (especially the Eucharist) and guard and pass on the tradition (the Gospel). In Acts 6.1–6, we read of the first extension of their office with the appointment of deacons (literally "servants"), to relieve the apostles of their routine work in order that they might be able to exercise their apostolic functions more freely. Presumably the work of the early deacons was not only to "serve tables," as Acts puts it, but also to act as the bishops' assistants in the administration of funds and the care of the poor and widows. Such, at any rate, was their later function, in addition to the duty of carrying the reserved sacrament from the Sunday Eucharist to those who were unable to be present.

Finally, another development took place. We can imagine that as the church became established in the centre of the cities, it rapidly began to push out into the countryside. One implication is obvious; the faithful found it increasingly difficult (and meaningless) to be part of a community far from their homes. Many of them must have lived a day's walk or more from their nearest city. Inevitably Christian communities began to grow up in villages and towns, spreading farther and farther from the city centres. Who was to care for these new churches, and more specifically, who was to preside at their weekly Eucharist? Soon the bishop began to appoint priests or "presbyters" to look after them. He commissioned them by the laying-on of hands, giving them the delegated authority to lead the local congregation, celebrate the Eucharist, and absolve the people from their sins. They were to be responsible to their bishop for the pastoral care which they exercised on his behalf.

Such were the beginnings of the Christian ministry. Much later, the ecclesiastical map came to be split up into divisions and sub-divisions called dioceses and parishes, corresponding to similar administrative divisions within the Roman Empire. The Empire eventually collapsed, but the pattern has been preserved into our own day with the bishop as pastor of the diocese and the priest being responsible for the parish unit.

Persecution. The first three centuries were heroic days in the church's life, when Christians lived under the constant threat of persecution. In the Roman Empire it was compulsory to worship the emperor as God. Because of their belief in a unique God, the Jews had been exempt from this requirement, but no one else was. So when the new Christian faith was disowned by its Jewish parent, its followers were faced with the full demand of the law. But the followers of Christ clearly could not worship the emperor. Jesus alone was Lord, and they considered it blasphemy to pay divine respect to any man.

Christians almost immediately found themselves practising an illegal religion, one whose leader (Jesus) had been executed as a suspected revolutionary. People claimed that his followers had stirred up trouble wherever they had gone in the Jewish world. The result was three hundred years of persecution, and the necessity for Christians to become fugitives and often fear for their lives. Persecution was not always active — indeed, there were long periods of comparative peace when the law was not applied. But Christians were always under suspicion, and at the least excuse, fierce persecution might break out. It began under the mad emperor Nero (A.D. 50) in Rome, during whose time thousands of Christians were killed. Somewhat later, in A.D. 110, we have a record of official correspondence between the provincial official and the emperor about how the persecution was to be applied in Bithynia, a region of Asia Minor.[22] We also have a moving series of letters written by Ignatius, a bishop of the same region, while he was being taken under guard to his eventual death in the arena.[23] Such records give us an idea of the high cost of being a Christian in those early days.

Official persecution continued intermittently for three centuries, creating a tough church, schooled under hardship and producing many martyrs. One of its most notable legacies is the list of those who gave their lives for Christ in this period, and whose days of commemoration led to the growth of the Christian calendar. A revised edition, updated and simplified, is to be found between pages ix and xii of the Anglican Prayer Book, and a further revision, emphasizing even more current and regional names, is the work of the Doctrine and Worship Committee.

Worship in this period was inevitably flexible and varied. The focus of worship in the new church was of course the Eucharist, in obedience to our Lord's command at the Last Supper to "do this" in order to recall his presence. Faithfully, Sunday by Sunday, the first Christians "did this" and knew the presence of the risen Lord among them. Initially, the Eucharistic celebration was a real meal like all the other suppers which Jesus had shared with his followers. However, as the celebration spread into the non-Jewish environment, the meal was omitted, and the Eucharist assumed the basic form which those of us who use revised modern liturgies would recognize.

From the record left by Justin (a Roman teacher, A.D. 150), the procedure was extremely simple.[24] The members came together at the appointed time, greeted each other, listened to some readings, and prayed for God's world and his church. Bread and wine were presented; the president took them and blessed them, broke and shared them with all present. Then everyone was dismissed and they all went home. This would have been a simple affair, conducted in someone's back room or in a safe place where soldiers would not disturb or come to arrest them. There would have been a good deal of impromptu praying and the singing of psalms and hymns. Although Justin does not mention it, there is every reason to believe that there would have been such spiritual signs as healing and prophecy, as well as fellowship and sharing.

As time went on, these liturgies (literally "work of the people") naturally became more formalized, but there was no uniformity. Inevitably, because man is a creative animal, certain prayers and hymns came into regional use. Some of these have come down to us in such hymns as the Gloria in Excelsis or the Agnus Dei (Prayer Book pages 86 and 84). But the picture is essentially one of variety and flexibility.

Thought. The very first Christians had to put a prodigious amount of thought into interpreting the life and work of Jesus. This thinking did not stop with the writing of the New Testament. It went on unabated. Sometimes it wandered into channels which led far from the Apostolic teaching; even Saint Paul warned his followers about false teachers who were perverting and twisting the faith.

Over the years many perversions of the Gospel developed. These were called "heresies" or false teachings; they were so called in distinction to "orthodoxy" (which means literally "true teaching"). Nearly all of these early heresies had to do with the nature of Jesus. They swung between the teaching that Jesus was only a spirit and not really human (Docetism, which flourished in the second century), and the opposite heresy that he was only a *man*, albeit a very holy one. This teaching was condemned by the Church in A.D. 268 but later revived in a refined form by Arius. The Arian heresy threatened to split the church and led to the calling of the first great ecumenical Council at Nicaea in A.D. 325.

Another heresy, taught by a man called Montanus, overemphasized the person of the Holy Spirit. This resulted in an often bizarre exaltation of prophecy as the only real mark of the Christian. A whole cluster of heresies was caused by the influence of "Gnostic" teaching, which was very deeply rooted throughout the Roman Empire at the time when the early church was spreading. Gnosticism is a difficult philosophy to describe, but as its name implies (the Greek word *gnosis* means knowledge), its strength lay in people's attraction to cults which teach special mysterious and secret knowledge. It had great appeal, but was vigorously opposed by the early Christian thinkers from Saint Paul onward.

It was as much to fight against such false teachings as it was to continue the process of interpretation, that Christian theology developed rapidly during those first three hundred years. The period abounds with the names of famous "doctors" of the church, who laid the basis for subsequent theologians. One of their goals was to interpret the faith to the thinking men and women of their own day. To do this, they attempted to explain Christianity in terms of the current ideas taught by the philosophers. One such thinker whose ideas dominated the intellectual world at that time was the Greek philosopher Plato. The Christian theology that emerged from this period included many Platonic ideas, and represents one of the most brilliant attempts ever made to convey the truths of the Gospel in terms of contemporary culture. Those who are interested in following this up might well study the writings of such teachers as Clement and Origen, who wrote at the beginning of the third century A.D. from Alexandria, then the greatest seat of learning in the world.

Another expression of this concern to counter heresy and interpret the faith was the creation of the three great creeds of the church, although they were not officially formulated until after the first three centuries. Two were originally local baptismal creeds which were to be said by all candidates for baptism. They were eventually accepted at a series of ecumenical councils as authoritative statements of the faith, believed by the whole church.

The *Apostles' Creed* was the earliest. It was not, as the name implies, written by the apostles, but was given this title because it was believed to summarize the faith handed down by the first apostles. (*Apostolic*, in this sense, was understood to mean orthodox or authentic.) Probably the original baptismal creed of the church of Rome, it crystallized in its present form during the fourth century.

The *Nicene Creed* was not, despite the name, the creed of the church or Council of Nicaea! It was called the Nicene Creed because it was a further definition of the nature of Christ which had been the subject of so much debate at that council. Probably based on the baptismal creed of the church in either Jerusalem or Caesarea, it was further refined as a result of the Council of Nicea. The Nicene Creed was composed in order to define quite specifically the humanity and divinity of Jesus. (Hence the phrases: "God of God, Light of Light, true God from true God . . . being of one substance with the Father," etc.). It was intended to answer the heresy of Arianism for good. Its formal acceptance is associated with the Council of Constantinople (A.D. 381).

The *Athanasian Creed* (Prayer Book page 695) was not the work of Saint Athanasius but a product of the Western church. It bears his name because it represented his explicit definition of the nature of Christ, which he had argued against Arius at the Council of Nicaea. But the question of Christ's nature had not been fully settled even after the promulgation of the Nicene Creed. In an attempt to end argument and dissension three more councils were convened at Constantinople (A.D. 381), Ephesus (A.D. 431), and Chalcedon (A.D. 451) where the church finally formulated the doctrine, according to the teaching of Athanasius, that Christ was both "wholly God" and "wholly man." These three creeds and four great councils are thus responsible for the basic definitions of our faith and are so regarded by most Christians.

B The Established Church: from 312 until the Collapse of the Empire

In the year A.D. 312, an event of immense importance to the church took place. The emperor Diocletian died, and General Constantine was proclaimed emperor by the troops under his command. He was at that time in command of the Roman forces in Britain, and he immediately set out for Rome to secure the throne against the claim of a rival general. Now, the most important and unusual aspect of Constantine is that he was a Christian. He had been led to Christ by his British mother, and shortly before returning to Rome, he is said to have had a vision of a cross in the sky with the words "In this sign, conquer."

This is precisely what he did, winning the Battle of Milvian Bridge in A.D. 313. He was made emperor, and very rapidly Christianity became not only legal but the official religion of the Empire. The immediate effect on the church was obviously very joyful; it meant an end to three hundred years of terrifying persecution. Christians no longer needed to worship in secret and go about in fear, and church buildings began to appear everywhere, symbolizing the new freedom. But this was a mixed blessing. Under persecution it had not been easy to be a Christian; for many the way of the cross had been a frightening reality, and the years of struggle had produced a very tough and strong faith. Now all that was changed. It was suddenly fashionable to be a Christian, and people flocked to the new churches. "Social" Christianity was born. It could almost be said that the age of the "comfortable pew" was ushered in with the edict of Constantine!

Now another problem appeared — the relationship between the church and the state. For three hundred years the church had been separate and apart from the state. But one of the first acts of Constantine, when he had established himself as emperor, was to call an ecumenical council to meet with him at Nicaea in order to bring an end to the Arian dispute within the church. Here, for the first time, we see the state beginning to exert control over the church, and we see the church allowing itself to be patronized and protected by government. It was the beginning of a relationship fraught with problems.

The effects of this new twist to history were twofold. First, it led to the growth of nominal Christianity and a weakening of the church's original toughness; second, it set the scene for a continuing dispute over the respective powers of church and state.

The Growth of the Papacy. One result of the inevitable alignment of the church with the secular power was the increasing influence of the bishops of the two capital cities of the Empire. The heart of the Roman Empire, of course, had always been Rome, and so it continued to be. Because of the continuing unrest in the East, however, the new emperor deliberately set up a second capital in the city which was renamed Constantinople. Much of his time he spent in this second capital.

Inevitably the bishops of Rome and Constantinople (earlier called Byzantium) came to have overwhelming influence among their fellow bishops. The Roman bishop had always enjoyed a pre-eminence, partly because Rome was the imperial city, and partly because there the bones of Peter were said to reside. This was of great importance to the early Christians. However, from the time of Constantine onward, the prestige of these two bishops increased greatly, although not without opposition from fellow bishops, who frequently resented what they believed to be the unwarranted exercise of power.

This development is important in the light of later history, particularly in the West where the papacy came to have absolute power over the church. Ultimately the ecclesiastical power struggle between Rome and Constantinople became so great that, in A.D. 1054, they mutually excommunicated each other. This separation, known as the Great Schism, is still reflected in the broad division between Western Catholicism and the "Orthodox" Churches of the East.[25]

Monasticism. If the new freedom was welcomed by most people after centuries of fear and persecution, it soon came to be seen by others as a dangerous threat to the uncompromising demands of the Gospel. While the new and relative ease of the Christian life was no doubt good enough for the majority, it was met with deep suspicion by others. All around they felt standards slipping, as Christianity began to conform more and more to the values of the world. So, at first singly and then in growing numbers, some people began to opt out of the world and seek to follow a tougher and more ascetic life. They left their homes and occupations, and went to live in the deserts to lead lives of prayer, self-denial, and discipline.

By the fourth century, the numbers of these monks had grown enormously, and it became vital for them to be properly organized: They needed some kind of regulation in their lives, so that they might be properly disciplined and not left to work out their individual forms of spirituality and styles of living. Eventually such a "rule" was written by a monk later to be honoured as Saint Benedict (sixth century). This became the foundation of similar rules used by communities of monks throughout the church. It was a rule (or a "regulated" way of life) based on the threefold vows of poverty, chastity, and obedience, which every monk was obliged to take when entering the community. It also organized the life of each religious community around the recital of the "Daily Offices," services of psalms, readings, prayers, and hymns which were to be sung eight times a day. Several varieties of this basic rule were developed, depending upon whether the community's task was strictly limited to prayer or whether it embraced some form of active ministry. The monastic movement grew rapidly in the centuries following the days of Constantine, and was a potent factor in the expansion of the church in the centuries that were to follow the destruction of the Roman Empire.

C   Collapse of Empire: Opportunity for the Church (A.D. 450 to 1000)

The worldly glory of the new era which Constantine inaugurated was destined to collapse. By the end of the fourth century, barbarians from lands outside the Roman Empire were beginning to threaten the safety of the Empire, and in A.D. 410 the imperial city itself was sacked and burned by Alaric, the head of the barbarian invaders. In a very few years, the ancient and proud empire was in ruins and the world entered a period commonly known as the Dark Ages. The efficient administrative system of Rome collapsed, the army disintegrated, and the economy fell into ruin. Yet one of the few institutions which did not share in the general disruption was the church. Despite the destruction of her buildings, the killing of many of her leaders, and the removal of Christianity from many parts of the empire, the church survived and, in fact, began to enter another heroic age. In a sense, the only light that remained in the world was the light of Christ's church. And when the darkness lifted after years of decay, it was a Christian light, a Christian civilization which was diffused over the new world. In the opinion of many Christians of those later centuries, the old Roman Empire was replaced by a new Christian one. They even had a name for it — Christendom.

It is interesting to look at this heroic age from a peculiarly English (if not Anglican) viewpoint. The Catholic Church had been active in England since the second century, when we know that its first martyr, Saint Alban, had been murdered. When the Empire collapsed during the fifth century, most of England was overrun by barbarian invaders from across the North Sea. These pagan invaders stamped out Christianity, driving the survivors to the extreme west and across the sea to Ireland. In Ireland the church flourished, maintaining a connection with the continent. It was largely a monastic church, developing its own particular genus of Catholicism and producing some remarkable leaders. Eventually some of these missionary monks established a mission on Holy Island, on the coast of western Scotland, and another at Lindisfarne, in the north-east of England, hoping to be able to reconvert the rest of the country to Christ.

As it eventually turned out, England was won back to Christ by a missionary movement from the north and the south simultaneously. From Lindisfarne in the north came missionary priests like Saint Cedd, who sailed down the east coast in about A.D. 604 and landed on the lonely Essex marshes. He preached to the East Anglians and built a small stone church by the sea. (It still remains and is the scene of an annual diocesan pilgrimage.)

The slowly expanding church on the continent to the south began again to take note of the "barbaric" island in the north. Pope Gregory the Great felt that the time had come to attempt the reconversion of England; so in 596 he sent a monk called Augustine to effect this work. After turning back once and being duly rebuffed by Gregory, Augustine finally crossed the channel. To his relief and surprise, he found that the queen of the southern kingdom was already a believer. He succeeded in converting the king, whose subjects duly followed their monarch in coming forward for baptism. Augustine was given permission to build a church in Canterbury. After being consecrated bishop by the pope, Augustine took this small church to be his cathedral. His fellow missioner, Paulinus, was sent north, and soon he and Augustine found themselves the bishops of this reconverted country, governing it from the two cities of Canterbury and York.

There had been a danger in England that the Roman missioners might have clashed with those from the north. The latter, because of their greater isolation from the centre of affairs in Rome, had developed a strong sense of independence. (They had held out against the barbarians for nearly two hundred years.) But the clash did not occur. At the Council of Whitby in A.D. 606, the jurisdiction of Rome was recognized. As a mark of respect, the English church was permitted to keep its own liturgical tradition at a time when virtually all the other regional churches were being obliged to submit to the Roman rite, which the Pope regarded as a means of unifying the Western church.

It is worth making a final note of the importance of the monks in this second "heroic" age of the church. The role they played in Britain, and throughout Europe, in preserving the faith against the pagans, was of immense importance. And in the slow reconversion of Europe which took place between A.D. 500 and 900, it was the monks who led the way. By the end of this period, a Christian civilization had spread across Europe, and the church was very much established in a position of great power.

D   The Mediaeval Church (A.D. 1000 to 1520)

The subject of the mediaeval church is vast, and many volumes have been written about it. All we can do is touch on a few significant aspects to grasp something of its great strengths and weaknesses. By the year 1000, the church had attained enormous temporal power. Herein lay the cause not only of its greatest achievements but also of its disastrous disintegration at the time of the Reformation, five hundred years later.

On the credit side of the mediaeval church, many things could be listed. Certainly the most lasting are the great architectural monuments it has left, not only in the cathedrals and abbeys of Europe but also in the thousands of parish churches in the towns and countryside, which still stand as symbols of the glory of God. They expressed not so much the economic power of the church, as the genuine piety and devotion of the thousands of benefactors who paid for the buildings. Together with the architecture must go the religious art, and later, the superb music of the Middle Ages. When mediaeval man wanted to do or create something beautiful, he often did it in the religious idiom and to the greater glory of his God.

The mediaeval church also saw the flowering of philosophy and theology, after centuries of comparative barrenness during the Dark Ages. A great burst of energy in the eleventh century issued in the founding of such great universities as Bologna, Paris, Cambridge, and Oxford. Within a new context of learning, the Christian Gospel was interpreted according to the modes of thought of the day. The Greek philosopher Aristotle had recently been rediscovered, and Thomas Aquinas, one of the greatest minds of all time, worked to redefine Christianity according to the framework of Aristotle's ideas. So influential was his work that a whole system of theology (called Scholasticism) was based on it. Scholasticism was to dominate Catholic thought until as recently as the 1960s.

The inner or spiritual life of the mediaeval church enjoyed several movements of renewal which left their mark on subsequent history. The monastic movement grew immensely strong, and these centuries saw a flowering of prayer and mysticism. The writings of such mystics as Saint John of the Cross, Thomas à Kempis, and Meister Eckhart still sell as popular paperbacks today. Some of this spiritual fervor was directed outward in attempts to reform both the church and society as a whole. The two best known movements were named after their founders, Saint Francis and Saint Dominic. Both movements reacted against dangers threatening the church. Francis fought to counter a spirit of worldliness and ease; Dominic to stem the spread of heresy. Both of these saints were intensely evangelistic and rooted out the complacency of the church from top to bottom. Another lesser known movement was called the Beguines. These were lay people who led otherwise normal working lives, but lived together in communities and followed a simple rule of prayer, good works, and the sharing of possessions. The Beguines were not always popular with the hierarchy because of their independence from formal control, but they continued from the thirteenth century right up to the eve of the Reformation.

The routine life of the mediaeval church went on in monasteries, cathedrals, and in thousands of parish churches, all with their own lay brothers, sisters, or clergy. This pattern is probably familiar to most of us, although not so ideal as many would imagine. The sacraments were dispensed, although actual communion by the laity was infrequent; sermons were preached, although not regularly, for many of the clergy had simply not been trained to do so; the daily offices were sung in the monasteries; the poor were looked after, although only in the more conscientious parishes and religious houses; the luckier children were taught the rudiments of Latin and religion; people learned about Christ and went to their graves in hope of eternal life.

Yet seeds of decay were apparent for those who had eyes to see them. The braver and more articulate church people cried out against wrong. The abuses and corruption that usually go with great power were threatening the Body of Christ. Bishoprics were too often given as rewards for political service, or used as bribes for political support. Men would be made rectors of several parishes without even visiting them; they simply paid a poor priest a pittance to make sure that the statutory services were provided. Inevitably the poor priest would be badly educated, he rarely preached, and was as full of superstition as many in his flock. Clerical marriage was forbidden, yet it was not uncommon for a parish clergyman to be living with a woman. Bishops sired children and gave them rectories as a source of income.

The cost of maintaining both the fabric and the bureaucracy of the church became increasingly onerous. So new and more demanding systems were devised to tax the people at the base of the church. Now, the idea that all the people should be expected to share in the costs of church administration might be defended, but the systems devised to do this were often of dubious morality. Most notorious was the system of selling "indulgences": in exchange for a money payment, the church promised that the giver would have a number of days remitted from his "sentence" in purgatory. (Purgatory was the name given to the place or process by which the soul would be purified or purged before it was fit to enter heaven.) "Pay now and you'll have ten years less to serve later!" Such was popular credulity that the indulgence seller did a thriving trade and the money flowed in.

During the years A.D. 1000 to 1500, the mediaeval church grew steadily more corrupt and in need of change. John Wycliffe, who preached reform in the fourteenth century in England, was branded a heretic. He was banned from Oxford and exiled to a country parish, where he died in 1384. His bones were disinterred and burnt in 1428. The preacher Savanarola bravely defied the authorities in his native Florence, and was burned at the stake. Yet the winds of change continued to blow. A new spirit of criticism began with the rediscovery of ancient learning associated with the Renaissance. The Bible was translated into the common language of the people, although this had been forbidden by the church lest it encourage free-thinking and heresy. And the invention of printing ensured that the new translations would get into an increasing number of hands. People who read their Bibles began to judge what they saw around them in the light of what they read. Intelligent and enquiring readers, like Erasmus, began to ask questions and demand reforms. The Pope appeared to listen to such complaints, and called a council of the Western church to meet at Constance (Switzerland) in 1414. But after listening to the recommendations, the Pope did virtually nothing. Inevitably the head of steam grew powerful and eventually blew the calm and unity of the Catholic Church to pieces. The Reformation began.

E   The Reformation (16th Century)

The word *Reformation* is a misnomer. It was in fact an ecclesiastical revolution which destroyed the unity of Western Christendom and gave birth to what came to be called Protestantism. It began, appropriately enough, with a protest. Martin Luther, a monk of the Germany city of Wittenburg, heard that a certain John Tetzel, a well-known indulgence seller, was coming to the city in order to sell his wares. Luther seized the opportunity to make a list of ninety-five particular ecclesiastical abuses which he thought needed correcting, and he nailed the list to the door of the church where Tetzel would be preaching. When Tetzel read the complaint, he immediately took the list back to Rome and brought it to the attention of the Pope. It had been Luther's rather naive hope that, when the Pope read the document, he would be moved to do something to correct the abuses and reform the church. But he was wrong. The Pope's reply was a detachment of militia armed with a warrant for Luther's arrest. Hearing this, Luther escaped and appealed to the ruler of his local principality, the Elector of Saxony, for protection. He agreed to Luther's request and a full-scale religio-political war erupted; the northern principalities of Germany supported

Luther against the full weight of the southern imperial forces of the Holy Roman Empire. The northern princes saw this as a timely political opportunity to strike for their independence against the central power of the emperor, while the latter was fighting to retain control of his slowly disintegrating empire.

Other countries were rapidly drawn into the struggle, the southern countries of Europe coming to the defence of a political status quo which they favoured, the northern countries looking for a chance to further their growing national ambitions. In all this the Pope saw himself as the defender of the true faith and unity of the Catholic Church, while Luther and his growing followers believed they were fighting for the reform (although increasingly the overthrowal) of an institution which had grown corrupt and perverted.

Behind the political battle lines, another struggle was being fought by the contending forces within the church. What had begun as a protest against corruption and a plea for reform, rapidly broadened into a split which raised deep questions about the very meaning of the church herself and the nature of man's salvation. At the risk of generalization, the fundamental question eventually raised by Luther was this: where did the church fit into God's plan for man's salvation? Was salvation a private matter between each man and his God, depending solely upon that person's faith, or was it consequent upon his membership in the church and the regular use of the church's sacraments? Most of us would reject such an ''either . . . or'' type of question today, but it was one which faced the protagonists of the Reformation because of the critical nature of the situation.

Luther, followed by other European reformers, chose the former answer: each man was saved by his personal faith. This meant that the institutional church was not *essential* to salvation, although it was obviously desirable that individual Christians should meet together to study and share their faith. People were assured of salvation on the grounds of their personal faith in Christ, and were encouraged to desert the Catholic Church. Henceforth, they met in congregations to hear the teaching of the new reformers. It goes without saying that this meant a rejection of the Pope (who had failed to put his house in order) and the sacramental ministry of the Catholic Church. The new congregations worked out their own means of organization and chose their own "ministers," who might or might not have been former priests.

In essence the two opposing perspectives could be described as follows.

The Old Way

Salvation is achieved through the church and its sacraments.

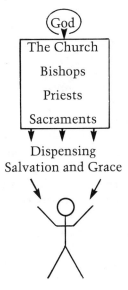

The Protestant Understanding

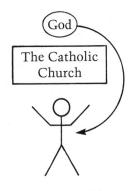

Salvation directly through a personal relationship with God by faith.
The Catholic Church is bypassed.

Question: What, then, is the church?

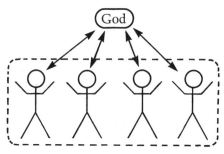

Protestant Answer: The church is now a loose association of individual Christians, each personally saved by our Lord.

The theological complexities behind such an apparently simple set of diagrams are considerable. Neither position was, in fact, quite as rigid as it appears and, in retrospect, neither stands on its own as a complete explanation of what it means to be a Christian. The "service centre" model of the Catholic Church, dispensing salvation and grace *regardless* of the personal faith of each individual, is a gross distortion of Catholic teaching. On the other hand, few Protestants would agree that the church is a "mere association." Yet the diagrams illustrate the broad lines of argument which were to divide the church for centuries.

Were sacraments necessary in the new order? Opinions differed among the reformers. Conservatives, like Martin Luther, held that sacraments were necessary, and so in the more conservative Lutheran Churches they are still retained. The more extreme reformers, however, saw them as unnecessary, if not actually unwarranted. John Calvin, the inspirer of today's Reformed and Presbyterian Churches, held them to be less important than did Luther. Zwingli, a Swiss reformer, went further than Calvin. The Society of Friends (or Quakers) dispensed with them entirely and saw each man in a personal, spiritual contact with his God by prayer and meditation.

On the continent of Europe, the close of the religious wars left a divided church. Spain, Italy, and what are now Austria, Hungary, and southern Germany, remained staunchly in communion with Rome. The northern countries became, in varying degrees, Protestant. Northern Germany saw the establishment of a new Lutheran Church, as did the countries of Scandinavia. France was affected by Calvin's teaching and Switzerland by Zwingli's. Although each of these countries was eventually won back to Catholicism by political force, the seeds of the "reformed" churches had been planted. The Low Countries (Holland and Belgium) were eventually to be divided along religious lines, the Dutch and Flemish peoples becoming Protestant while the French remained Catholic. In many of the Protestant countries, the more extreme groups of Baptists and Quakers took root and gathered congregations. The old unity of Christendom and the Catholic Church was shattered.

10

The English Church — at Home and Abroad

A   Reform in England

Where did the Church in England fit in all this upheaval? Was it Catholic or Protestant? Did it begin anew with Henry VIII? How did Anglicanism come into being? These are the questions we ask today when we are looking for our roots.

The Church of England did not begin with Henry VIII. It started in the first or the second century and remained for 1500 years as part of the Western Catholic Church. At the time of the Reformation, the English Church removed itself from the jurisdiction of the papacy and carried out a series of internal reforms (most of which have since been carried out within Roman Catholicism as a result of Vatican II). But it remained the same Catholic Church of the country with largely the same clergy.

Let us look at this in some detail. When Luther first challenged the authority of the Pope, Henry VIII in England condemned him and was duly rewarded by the Pope with the title of *Fidei Defensor* (Defender of the Faith — a title which used to appear on all British coinage as the abbreviation Fid.Def.). However, Henry's political problem resulting from his wife Catherine's failure to produce a male child, led him to request the Pope for an annulment on the grounds that she had been formerly married to his elder brother Arthur. This would then leave him free to remarry, have a male child, and so ensure the succession of the English throne. But the Pope was in no position to grant the request because he was effectively the prisoner of Catherine's nephew the emperor, whose troops were surrounding Rome. Henry took advantage of the timely death of his archbishop to appoint another who agreed to grant him dispensation despite opposition from Rome. As a result the Pope broke communion with Henry and the English Church.

In response, Henry began increasingly to take political (although not spiritual) control of the English Church. He stopped sending taxes to Rome, secularized the monasteries, and declared himself head of the Church in England. It is important to note that this move was aimed at gaining political control of the church, its finances and its appointments, in England. The church at that time exercised considerable political power. In no way was Henry's action an attempt to interfere with its spiritual life. He continued to regard the reformist teachings with disapproval and, in his lifetime, took care that the Church in England would remain firmly Catholic in its teaching, faith, and practice, although not in communion with Rome.

When he died in 1547, his son, the young Edward VI, became king and immediately fell under the influence of his "protectors." They were men of extreme reformist tendencies. During Edward's short reign of six years, the Church in England was increasingly affected by the new Protestant teaching. However, on Edward's death in 1553, his sister Mary Tudor became queen. Mary was the religious opposite of Edward; she was a determined papist who was passionately concerned to restore the English Church to unity with Rome. The changes of Henry's and Edward's days were abolished, the Pope's authority was restored, and a wave of opposition to all reforming ideas swept the country. The pendulum had swung back violently to the other extreme. The political and religious stability of England was threatened, and the country held its breath.

When Mary died suddenly in 1558, Elizabeth became queen and the crucial question arose — which side would she favour? The country was divided. Would she preserve Mary's fanatically papal stance, or would she sweep the country into the arms of the reformers, who were anxious to come back into power? The stability of England rested on her decision. Elizabeth took neither course; she adopted what came to be the classic English remedy of compromise. In the highly charged atmosphere of 1559, the English Church strove to maintain its old established heritage, but as under Henry, it claimed freedom from the Roman jurisdiction and the right to make its own domestic reforms. Elizabeth acted accordingly. Supported by the overwhelming majority of her subjects, she claimed the right of the

English Church to autonomy, and declared herself as its temporal head. The Pope responded by excommunicating Elizabeth and placing the country under interdict, forbidding the sacraments to all who did not declare their submission to Rome. Although the interdict eventually ceased to be effective, the consequent separation from Rome remains to this day.

With the confirmation of independence, a number of reforms were made concerning the discipline and forms of worship to be followed by the church. The English Prayer Book, which had first been issued in Edward's reign, was further revised and authorized for use. We have noted that although this book was written in English, the basic forms of service were largely reformulations of the old Latin Mass and the daily offices of the priest. The old was not rejected, but rather reformed. This was to be the keynote of the changes now taking place. The translation of the old Latin service books was completed, clergy were permitted to marry, the Bible was officially translated, and people were encouraged to read it. Many corruptions and superstitions of the old mediaeval church were also removed, and steps were taken to improve the education of the clergy and to teach the people.

Was this reformed Church of England to be Catholic or Protestant? The question is confusing, largely because the words mean different things to different people. The English Church was certainly "Protestant" in that it "protested" against the absolute power of the Pope and the alleged corruptions of the Roman Church. But if Protestant means adhering to the new radical theology outlined above, then the English Church has never been Protestant. Nor, again, was it a new church, born at the Reformation (although for the first time it was formally called the "Church of England"). It was the old, but reformed, Catholic English Church that had existed for 1400 years. The following diagram may help to outline the balance between the forces of Catholicism and Reform, and explain how the fundamentally Catholic faith was preserved while long-needed reforms were brought about in the church during the reign of Elizabeth.

Ingredients

Catholic	Reformed
Retention of traditional liturgical worship (Eucharist, matins, evensong).	Separation from Rome. Prayers in English. Bible translated and propagated.
Retention of the sacraments.	Freedom of clergy to marry.
Retention of the orders of bishop, priest, and deacon (fundamental matters of faith, order, and worship).	Abolition of religious orders (restored in nineteenth century).
	Stress on teaching to dispel ignorance and superstition (changes in jurisdiction and discipline).

This Elizabethan settlement was naturally resisted by the Pope, who proceeded to release all who did not agree with it from their allegiance to the queen. This forced many otherwise peaceable subjects into becoming potentially treasonous. A period of plotting, persecution, and discrimination against Roman Catholics followed, leaving a legacy of mutual suspicion that has continued to the present century.

The Elizabethan compromise held together in England for about a hundred years. But the disruption of the Civil War (1643-1649), followed by the restoration of Charles II, brought further division. The more radical reformist elements, which Elizabeth had managed to placate in 1559, split away in 1660 to form the "Non-Conformist" Churches — so called because their members refused to conform to the Act of Uniformity of 1661 which obliged all people to worship in their own parish churches. The Non-Conformists gave rise to the Congregationalist, Baptist, and Quaker movements which soon moved across the Atlantic to the New World.

A century later the Industrial Revolution sapped the vitality of the Church in England. Millions of people were drawn into the new industrial centres of England, and were totally ignored and untouched by the parish clergy of their day. Because of the contemporary system of pew rents, the poor were virtually excluded from worship in many churches. Into this scene, in 1739, broke the young and ardent John Wesley, an English priest who had experienced a conversion that changed his whole life. Convinced that he was called by God to preach the Gospel to the mass of unchurched people, Wesley rode the length and breadth of England carrying the good news to the poor, encouraging them to repent and lead new lives, characterized by holiness and Godly discipline or "method." They listened to him with awe and responded with enthusiasm. Tragically the bishops and clergy turned their back on him. Rejected in most of the parish churches, Wesley encouraged the people to organize themselves under lay leaders and preachers. But this was not enough; the people were still hungry for the sacraments. Wesley implored the bishops to ordain some of his new leaders as priests to serve the new congregations, especially those in North America. They refused; so Wesley took it upon himself to ordain them. Because the church could not recognize as priests these men who had not been ordained by a bishop, separation inevitably resulted. The Methodist Church was born.

Thus, by the mid-eighteenth century the "mainline" churches, so familiar in the English-speaking world, had already come into being and were transplanted to the new soil of America and Canada. But the Church of England was still to receive two very powerful injections which have left their marks on Anglican life today. I am speaking of what are loosely called the "high" and the "low" church traditions; more accurately they should be termed Anglo-Catholic and Evangelical.

The rise of Methodism had certainly affected the Church of England. Within the parent church, Methodism sowed the seeds of a revival movement which was to shake the church out of her stupor in the mid-nineteenth century. Charles Simeon, John Newton, and William Wilberforce led a new wave of enthusiasm which seized the church and put great emphasis on preaching the Gospel and personal salvation through Jesus Christ. This came to be called the Evangelical Movement. Beginning with the leaders in the universities, it spread throughout the country. People were encouraged to study their Bibles and pray together, they flocked to listen to famous preachers, and the standard of preaching inevitably went up in many parish churches. Also the British Empire was expanding rapidly, and the eyes of the people were opened to the challenge of preaching the Gospel to the "heathen" in foreign lands. The native peoples of Africa and India became the targets of evangelical enthusiasm, just as the industrial masses in England became the objects of concern and good works. Missionaries, funded by the new missionary societies, were sent abroad with Bibles. At home, Sunday schools were started, tracts were handed out to the poor, and new interest was taken in social reform.

At the same time another movement was born, sparked by a sermon from a priest in an Oxford church. John Keble's sermon "On the National Apostasy" protested against Parliament claiming too much authority in church affairs. It was an appeal for the church to shake herself free from the state, a claim that the church was a divine institution at liberty to order her own life. As the debate continued, a group in Oxford began to draw attention to the Catholicity of the English Church, stating that it was part of the Western Catholic Church, and not simply a puppet of the English state. This "Oxford" or "Anglo-Catholic" Movement continues to influence Anglicanism today, representing the voice of Catholicism within the Anglican Church, reminding its members of their Catholic heritage. The movement stresses that the church is not a creation of the Protestant Reformation, and that the ministry, sacraments, and Catholic traditions are part of its essence.

The two movements were popularly called low and high church. Low churchmen promoted preaching, conversion, and the need for a personal relationship with Jesus Christ; high churchmen expressed their concerns most visibly in their emphasis upon colour and ceremony in worship — for this they were sometimes called "ritualists." But the most important contribution of the Anglo-Catholics has been their understanding of the nature of the church, her sacraments, and her spiritual life, particularly in disadvantaged industrialized urban centres. Over the last fifty years, there has been a very healthy cross-fertilization between these two movements, and today's Anglican Church has been profoundly affected by them both.

B The World

When the rapid spread of European influence throughout the world reached its peak during the last century, the Christian church inevitably enjoyed a parallel expansion. This is clearly a vast subject, so I shall confine myself to some observations about North America and the growth of the Anglican Communion.

The original French and English settlers in North America imported their own religious version of the division and developments that had already taken place in Europe. To the New World came the Roman Catholics of France and, later, some refugee Huguenots (Protestants) escaping Catholic persecution. From England came large numbers of Anglicans, who formed the majority of the settlers in the thirteen colonies and Canada. Dutch Calvinists were already putting down roots in New Amsterdam (New York), and they were joined in New England by English Non-Conformists from Baptist, Congregationalist, and Quaker backgrounds. Increasing numbers of Scottish settlers crossed the Atlantic, bringing their Presbyterian faith with them. (The Presbyterian Church of Scotland had been founded by the fiery preacher John Knox, who had been taught by Calvin in Europe.) Then in the eighteenth century came a wave of Methodists who carried their enthusiasm into the New World and sparked off a series of similar revivalist movements. These new beliefs fed the new lands.

For many years the Church of England in Canada attempted to retain its privileged position as the established church, and gained limited support from England. Such a position was unrealistic in the new country, with scores of Lutheran, Roman Catholic, Orthodox, and many other denominations all immigrating. We now have a "pluralistic" situation in Canada, with many different Christian churches, all equal under the law.

Meanwhile, the Church of England had wakened from its eighteenth century stupor to find that explorers and traders from England were opening up vast tracts of land all over the world. In some of these lands, the British were to settle and develop new nations. In others their influence was to be strong even though their tenure was more limited. In both instances the church saw the opportunity to minister to the needs of English settlers in countries such as Canada and Australia, as well as a chance to convert the native peoples, especially in the great continent of Africa.

Missionary societies were formed to solicit money from Christians in England in order to organize and pay for missionary work abroad. (The Church Missionary Society, the Universities Mission to Central Africa, and the South American Missionary Society come to mind.) Enthusiastic young men and women were eager to offer themselves as priests, doctors, teachers, and nurses for these new colonies. From our cynical point of view, it is easy to belittle these missionaries as misguided colonialists and paternalists. Yet the death rate in equatorial Africa, in particular, was horrifying, and nearly all of these people left comfortable homes for lives of considerable hardship and deprivation.

The Church of England in these places grew and multiplied, although it remained under control from England. In countries such as Canada and Australia, increasing control was demanded and won from the English hierarchy, until self-government was granted. In tropical countries, the life of newly-emerging churches remained directly governed through the missionary societies in England, as the bishops of these new churches were directly responsible to the Archbishop of Canterbury. This situation lasted until after the Second World War, when what we now call the Anglican Communion came into being. During the forties and fifties the regional churches gradually became autonomous. For example, there is now the Church of the Province of Central Africa and the Holy Catholic Church of Japan, each fully self-governing, with their own synods and bishops. About this time the title of "Church of England in Canada" was also dropped in favour of the new name of "The Anglican Church of Canada."

Yet this does not mean that the Anglican Church has been divided. What is now called the "Anglican Communion" is in fact a family of sister churches in communion with each other and linked by common tradition, faith, sacraments, and ministry. It is one church. To preserve this unity, all bishops of the Anglican Communion meet for the Lambeth Conference every ten years (1978 was the last) in order to preserve a consensus of faith and practice. The Anglican Consultative Council (a much smaller body) meets in the intervening five years; the Archbishop of Canterbury has no jurisdiction over any other bishops, although he is certainly regarded as a kind of spiritual head. The Anglican executive officer, a bishop, is responsible for the continuing relationship between the different churches within the Communion.

11

The Anglican Church of Canada: How It Works

One of the responsibilities of being a member of the Anglican Church of Canada is to know something of how it works, how its life is regulated and its decisions are made. I suspect that the great majority of Anglicans today are not well-informed about these matters. Is the Anglican Church ruled from the top by its bishops — or even by the Archbishop of Canterbury? Is it a democratic institution? How big a part does bureaucracy play? And what about its connections with the state? Are its clergy paid out of taxes, as in Sweden, for example? Does the government help pay for church buildings, as in France? In other words, how does the Anglican Church of Canada really *work*? The church functions in three different ways simultaneously. We will consider each of them separately, although in practice, of course, they all operate at the same time. I shall call them the episcopal, the democratic, and the administrative models.

A The Episcopal Model

As we read in Chapter 10, the church that emerged from the very early days was an episcopal church — its leaders were bishops who saw themselves as carrying on the role originally undertaken by the apostles. The bishops believed they were specially consecrated as heads of each regional church and, as such, were the representatives of Christ himself. In particular, they adopted a number of specific functions. As leaders of each local church, they were together responsible for the unity of the whole church (very soon to be called the Catholic Church). Within their own dioceses, therefore, they represented this universal church. In addition, they saw themselves as the guardians of the true (or orthodox) faith of the church. This was particularly important in the centuries following Christ, when the orthodox faith came under severe attack from a number of heretical movements. In short, the bishops became responsible for the government of the church and were specifically charged with the unity, discipline, and orthodoxy of its members.

This working model of the church was preserved in its entirety by the Anglican Church at the Reformation, and in the course of time was transferred to Canada and all other parts of the world where the Anglican Church took root. As a result, the basic historical model of the Anglican Church in Canada is episcopal, and its structure illustrates this from *top to bottom*. This latter phrase is significant, for when we consider this episcopal model, we have to recognize that the authority is understood as flowing downward, from Christ himself as head of the church, through the bishops (the apostles' successors) and priests of the church. Here, in diagrammatic form, is how this model works in practice.

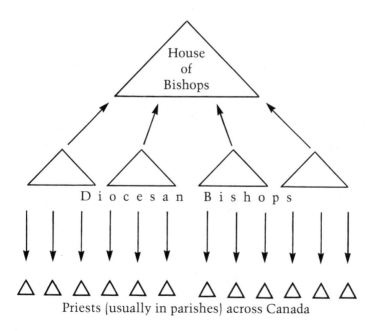

Priests (usually in parishes) across Canada

We have to start by recognizing that the fundamental unit in the Anglican Church is the diocese, with a bishop at its head. In Canada there are thirty dioceses, each with its own bishop. He has sole responsibility for the ordaining, appointing, and pastoral care of all his clergy; he is also responsible for the unity of his diocese and for all matters relating to doctrine. In practice this means that the bishop has the final voice in deciding whom he will ordain; he decides who goes to what parishes, and he has to deal with whatever pastoral problems there are among the clergy. He is the final arbiter in disputes and is the one who makes the final decisions on, for example, whether women should be made priests or young children admitted to Holy Communion. These are his functions within his own diocese.

However, because each diocese is only one part of a much larger church, all bishops in Canada meet periodically in the House of Bishops, presided over by the Primate (senior bishop). This body has no authority over each diocesan bishop, but it ensures that unity of faith and practice is maintained across the country. On an even higher level, these same bishops take part in the *Lambeth Conference.*

Moving down once more, the authority of the bishop is delegated to each priest both at his ordination and, in the case of all parish clergy, when he is inducted into his parish. Again the authority flows downward, and the priest enjoys in his parish much the same kind of authority as the bishop does in his diocese. It is interesting to note that, although a rector is paid by his parish and always works in co-operation with his parish council or vestry, he is answerable only to his bishop and is the authority in all matters of faith and order in his parish. In effect this means that he is responsible for such things as the worship of the parish, the preparation and admission of new Christians in baptism, who is confirmed, what is taught, and who does the teaching.

The episcopal model, then, has determined the basic structure of the church — its organization into dioceses and parishes. It is based upon the model of authority flowing downward from Christ to his bishops and, in turn, to each parish priest. It provides the framework for maintaining the worship and sacraments, the unity, and the teaching of the Catholic Church.

B The Democratic Model

In direct contrast is the democratic model, in which we might picture the authority as moving up rather than down. From the earliest times, the ordinary people (the laity) were recognized as having a vital part to play in governing the church. Even though the bishops were consecrated by their fellow bishops and thought of their commission as deriving directly from Christ, they were always appointed by the entire church, by the people as a whole. Sometimes they were acclaimed by the crowd (as in the case of the celebrated appointment of Saint Ambrose as Bishop of Milan), but more frequently by some kind of representative body. In many other areas of church government, the laity have always played an active part.

The most common way of involving the laity in the life and government of the church has been in synods. A synod is essentially a gathering of lay and clerical representatives to help or share with the bishop in conducting the affairs of the church. For many years this has been the model of the Anglican Church of Canada, and it has been applied at all three levels of the church's life: national, diocesan, and parochial. The following diagram will help to illustrate this more clearly.

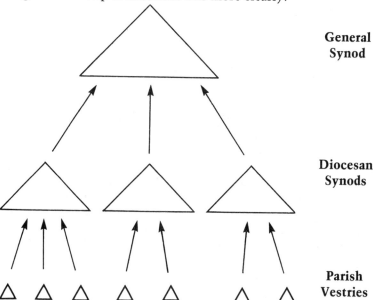

General Synod

Diocesan Synods

Parish Vestries

It would be simplest if we begin at the lowest level and move upward. Each parish elects its Vestry at the annual meeting. This usually consists of from one to three dozen members, and typically includes the leaders of the life and organizations of the parish. Within each parish, Vestry normally meets monthly and works with the rector and the two churchwardens in making many of the ongoing decisions of parish life. Legally, the actual authority in the parish is "vested" in the rector and wardens (called the "corporation"), but in practice this is often exercised by the larger elected body.

Also at the annual meeting, the parish elects several delegates to the Diocesan Synod, which meets every one to three years (for geographical reasons, the northern Diocesan Synods meet less frequently). It is in these Diocesan Synods that the most critical decisions of the church's life are made. This synod includes the bishop, the clergy, and the lay delegates of the diocese, and is concerned with the ongoing life of the diocese. It is responsible for decisions in most areas of its life, except those which are the bishop's prerogative. It does not, for example, tell the bishop whom he should ordain or whether children should be admitted to Holy Communion, although the bishop usually consults with the Diocesan Synod on matters such as these. It does, however, determine such things as the stipends of clergy, programs for the training of church school leaders, or whether new churches should be built in growing suburban areas.

In order to carry on the work of synod between its sessions, each diocese elects its Diocesan Council, which usually meets each month during the year. Synod also appoints a variety of committees and task forces to make sure that the more detailed work of the diocese is carried out during the year. A typical diocesan structure might be as illustrated on page 169.

Above the Diocesan Synods are two further levels, the Provincial and the National. The division of the larger church into (ecclesiastical) Provinces is very ancient. It came about due to the need for the bishops of any large region to come together in conference under the chairmanship of one of their peers, whom they appoint as archbishop. Canada is divided into four ecclesiastical Provinces: Canada (Quebec and the Maritimes), Ontario, Rupert's Land, and British Columbia. Periodically, representatives from the Diocesan Synods in these regions meet together to discuss things of regional or general concern. These Provincial Synods do not have any authority over the dioceses but can make recommendations for the dioceses to consider. Unlike the Diocesan Synods, those at the Provincial level rarely have any ongoing life between their sessions, and so it is unusual for a Provincial Synod to have committees corresponding to those at the diocesan level.

```
┌─────────────────┐
│     SYNOD       │
│ ┌─────────────┐ │
│ │   Council   │ │
│ └─────────────┘ │
└─────────────────┘
```

Administration And Finance	Program	Social Concerns	Planning	Ecumenism
	⊢Education		⊢Building Extension	
	⊢Counselling Services	⊢Refugees	⊢New Ministries	
	⊢Leadership Training	⊢Housing	⊢Etc., Etc.	
	⊢French Language Training	⊢Native Rights		AND
	⊢Etc., Etc.	⊢Etc., Etc.		OTHERS . . .

On top of all these is General Synod. Because of its growing importance over recent years, I shall spend somewhat longer looking at the way it works. The General Synod of the Anglican Church of Canada is sometimes likened to parliament, although there is a very important difference. Parliament is the highest legislative body in the country, making laws that apply throughout the land, but General Synod has no such powers, for the basic unit of the church's life remains in the diocese. General Synod can and does pass a great number of resolutions. It has, for example, stated its mind on such matters as capital punishment, abortion, or whether women should be admitted to the priesthood. But it cannot *impose* its decision on the whole church or do more than recommend specific courses of action to the dioceses. However, because it brings together Anglicans from across the country, General Synod does in a real sense speak for the entire Anglican Church in Canada.

General Synod meets every three years and includes the clergy and lay delegates from each of the Diocesan Synods. Like the other synods, it is composed of the three "houses" of bishops, clergy, and laity, so that all have their say in the national life of the church. Just like the Diocesan Synods, the General Synod gives birth to a bewildering array of committees, sub-committees, and task forces which continue its work between sessions. Here is a chart of its chief committees:

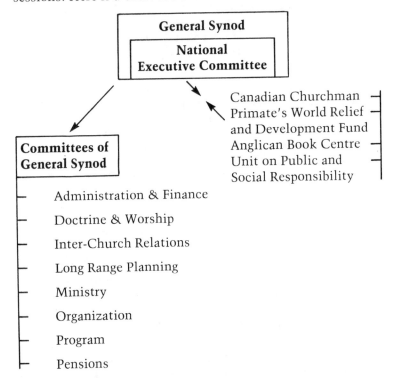

The National Executive Committee (NEC) carries on the work of General Synod when it is not in session. Chaired by the Primate, it is the centre of the church's nervous system. All the other sub-committees of synod report to the NEC at its quarterly meetings. These various sub-committees are made up of a mixture of clergy and laity appointed by General Synod. They usually meet quarterly and involve a large number of people from across the country so that all regions of Canada are included in the ongoing committee work of the church. Many of these committees give birth to still more sub-committees, commissions, and task forces! The Doctrine and Worship Committee, for example, selected special groups to work on new orders of service for marriage, burial, and Holy Communion; the Program Committee appointed a task force to examine the idea of a guaranteed annual income, while the Long Range Planning Committee was responsible for making projections regarding the longer-term shapes and needs of the church. In this way, even larger numbers of individuals are involved in the day to day work of the church at the national level.

As if all this were not enough, there are other activities which relate to General Synod, through the NEC. The *Canadian Churchman*, the national church newspaper, although enjoying complete freedom of operation and editorial policy, is ultimately responsible to this assembly. Although the former Anglican Church Women's organization is now phased out, there is a committee dealing directly with women's work which reports to General Synod. The Primate's World Relief and Development Fund is another such body. With the Primate as its chairman, it is responsible for the overseas aid and development work of the national church. Although it began as a means of handling money given in response to overseas disasters such as the crisis in Bangladesh, its concerns have expanded to embrace the much wider field of development, human rights, and refugees both abroad and here in Canada. The *Anglican Book Centre* also comes under the umbrella of General Synod; its work has grown considerably from simply running a bookstore in Toronto to providing a mail service across Canada and, more recently, developing its own publishing program.

One of the creations of General Synod which has attracted a good deal of support and criticism over the past few years has been the Unit on Public and Social Responsibility. This was formed in order to give expression for the church's inevitable concerns in such worldly spheres as politics, economics, and business. Because of its high profile activities in bank shareholders' meetings and its pronouncements on such issues as racism in South Africa or the dangers of nuclear proliferation, it has earned a lot of attention in both the secular as well as the religious press.

Under the banner of General Synod comes a broad variety of

activities embracing almost all aspects of the church's life, involving a cross-section of people from Newfoundland to the West Coast.

C   The Administrative Model

Just as the church has its episcopal and democratic ways of working, so it has its administrative machinery at all but the provincial levels. Again, it might be best if we see how this works at the lowest level, the local parish.

The parish staff may vary from the rector who does all his own typing, phoning, and filing in a small parish, to a much more varied administrative staff in a large city church. Usually a rector is assisted by a part- or full-time secretary; he may also have the services of a bookkeeper and other staff workers.

At the diocesan level the full-time staff vary according to the size (and wealth) of the diocese. A larger diocese may employ several clergy in executive and programming jobs, as well as a number of accounting and secretarial staff. The national headquarters of the Anglican Church of Canada is at 600 Jarvis Street, in Toronto. The building houses the Primate's Office and the Anglican Book Centre as well as a variety of departments on its four floors.

Its staff is divided into a number of departments or divisions which, to some extent, correspond to the chief committees of General Synod. This becomes clearer when we see them side by side.

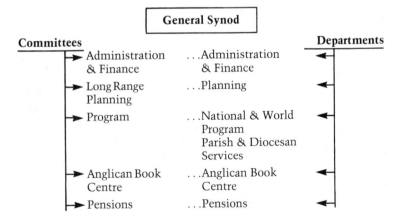

	General Synod	
Committees		**Departments**
Administration & Finance	...Administration & Finance	
Long Range Planning	...Planning	
Program	...National & World Program Parish & Diocesan Services	
Anglican Book Centre	...Anglican Book Centre	
Pensions	...Pensions	

These are the three basic "models" which help us to understand how the Anglican Church of Canada functions. The first describes the special responsibilities and work of the bishops and priests in their unique role as the leaders and pastors of the church. The second demonstrates how the church is also a democratic institution, with all its members having roles to play in moulding its life and sharing its decisions. The flow of power is not downward, as in the episcopal model, but from the bottom to the top. In both of these models, the diocese is the centre of authority and decision-making. In the third model, we see the administration at work, serving the church at the parish, diocesan, and national levels. In actual practice, of course, all three models work together more or less in harmony at each level, and this is where the picture can become more confusing. With the help of these models, however, the basic administrative structures may become clear.

How Does the Anglican Church of Canada Relate to Other Churches?

Let us take the simplest answer first. On both the parish and diocesan levels, there are many kinds of relationships which are constantly developing or declining between Anglican and other Christian Churches. Sometimes this takes place on an official footing, when for example they relate as fellow members of a local Council of Churches at the parish level. More often these relationships develop through one of a variety of informal associations. They frequently involve specific concerns, such as the organizing of days of prayer, or the Ten Days for World Development program (see below). Because so much of this activity is varied and informal, however, I do not attempt to elaborate on it.

At the national level, the relationships become much more formal, and a number of joint church bodies have emerged which are of considerable importance. Here is the picture.

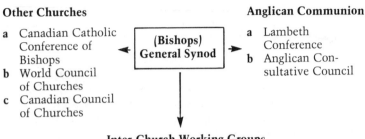

Other Churches

a Canadian Catholic Conference of Bishops
b World Council of Churches
c Canadian Council of Churches

(Bishops) General Synod

Anglican Communion

a Lambeth Conference
b Anglican Consultative Council

Inter-Church Working Groups

Inter-Church Committee on World Development
Inter-Church Committee on Population
Inter-Church Human Rights Task Force
Gatt-Fly
CICARWS (Commission on Inter-Church Aid, Relief and World Services)
Etc., Etc.

General Synod relates to the rest of the Anglican Communion in two ways. Every ten years, as we have seen, all the diocesan bishops from around the world meet to confer at the Lambeth Conference. Then, to make sure that this communication is kept open, our General Synod appoints representatives to the Anglican Consultative Council, which continues to meet in the intervening years.

Second, General Synod relates to many other Christian churches both in Canada and abroad. The bishops meet periodically with their Roman Catholic counterparts. General Synod, through its representatives, meets more formally with a much wider range of churches on both the World and the Canadian Council of Churches. All these meetings are largely consultative; however, there is also a changing number of working committees with members drawn from most of the Canadian churches, who work jointly on a variety of inter-church projects or issues. Some of these frequently achieve a high profile because of the topical nature of the work they are doing. *Gatt-Fly* (a play on words, deriving from the General Agreement on Tariffs and Trade and the insect called the gadfly) was created as a research group to advise the churches on matters of international trade, with particular respect to Third World countries. An Inter-Church Committee on World Development produces the annual "Ten Days" material, used by many churches to focus attention upon the needs of the world's poorest nations. The Human Rights Committee grew in response to the need for the churches to work together in this increasingly critical area. Another body with the formidable series of initials CICARWS (Commission for Inter-Church Aid, Relief and World Services) draws together the overseas aid committees of five major churches to ensure that there is no duplication in what they are doing, and in order that they can work together on joint development projects. The list of these committees continually changes as the churches respond to the need to work more effectively together.

In ways such as these, General Synod is able to relate, not only to Christians in other parts of the Anglican Communion, but also with many other Christian churches in our own country.

Where Does the Money Come From . . . and Go To?

First of all, let us do away with a popular misconception. The Anglican Church in Canada (or indeed in any other part of the world) does not receive money from the state. All its funds are raised from membership, either those who are living (in the form of regular giving), or those who have left money for endowments in their wills. Another point worth mentioning is that no money is received from the state for the upkeep of church buildings, although many of them are of great historical and architectural interest. In short, the church has to meet all its considerable costs from the giving of its members. The source of the money is fairly straightforward; where it all goes is harder to explain. The following diagram will help to make this clear.

Each dollar given is used to support the work of the church at a number of different levels. Out of all the money donated in a typical parish, the greater part is used in supporting its own life and ministry. The rector, the secretary, and the organist have to be paid, the buildings must be heated and kept in good repair, the church school has to be equipped, and the year's programs need to be funded. But a proportion of the funds — called the "apportionment" — is sent to the diocese.

The diocese pays all its expenses out of the collective apportionment from all of its parishes. It takes what it needs to pay the staff, run the "plant," and finance the various diocesan programs. Funds may be used, for example, to subsidize a marriage counselling program, a church school teachers' weekend, or a diocesan retreat. The amount in the budget naturally depends on the size and resources of the diocese.

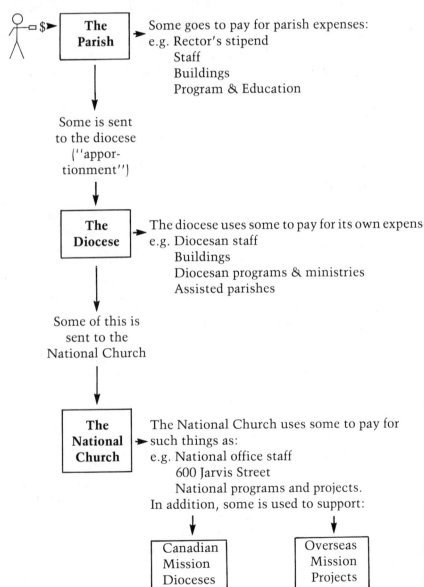

The Parish → Some goes to pay for parish expenses:
e.g. Rector's stipend
Staff
Buildings
Program & Education

Some is sent to the diocese ("apportionment")

The Diocese → The diocese uses some to pay for its own expens
e.g. Diocesan staff
Buildings
Diocesan programs & ministries
Assisted parishes

Some of this is sent to the National Church

The National Church → The National Church uses some to pay for such things as:
e.g. National office staff
600 Jarvis Street
National programs and projects.
In addition, some is used to support:

Canadian Mission Dioceses

Overseas Mission Projects

Out of its income from the parishes, the diocese then sends a portion to pay for all the expenses of the church at the national level. Here again are all the usual kinds of expenses. There is the Church House staff to pay and the costs of the building to meet. The considerable travelling expenses, which make it possible for people across Canada to meet, all have to be paid out of this budget, as do the costs involved in running the wide variety of national church programs and projects.

Yet this is still not the end of the story, for a large part of all the money received at the national level is in turn passed on to pay for mission work. Some of this work is in Canada, especially in the north, where it is impossible for the church to be self-supporting. The expenses faced by clergy living in the far north are extremely high, far above the capacity of the scattered population to support. The rest of the mission money is sent abroad to pay for projects of the Anglican Church of Canada, largely in Third World countries. One of the most important uses for mission money is the training of clergy and Christian workers in Uganda or the Caribbean. In all of these ways, the dollars that are given in church on Sundays are used to pay for a wide range of Christian work, beginning in the home parish but spreading outward to diocese, country, and world.

"Questions People Ask"

Of all the sessions I have ever had with adult study groups, by far the most popular has been the one to do with ecclesiastical extras — those things about which so many of us are puzzled. So it would be unfair if I did not add this appendix in order to deal with some of these odds and ends concerning our church and its life.

Here is a mixed collection of items to satisfy the curious. There is little attempt at logical order, other than listing in alphabetical sequence under headings. First we will deal with some items concerning worship.

Bowing, Genuflecting, and Crossing

At one time, these were the sure marks that one was a "high" churchman or an Anglo-Catholic. But they have now passed into general use in the church and are practised by many people, regardless of their one-time associations. I have grouped them because they are all forms of what we would now call "body language." There are means of communicating other than with the voice. A kiss, a handshake, a smile are all ways in which we "talk" to each other without speaking. Religion also has sign language which is used in worship and in our private devotions.

Bowing (the slight inclination of the head and shoulders) is a gesture of recognition, devotion, or thanks. In church one bows when moving in front of the altar (the symbol of God's presence) and at certain points in the liturgy, for example, at the name of Jesus. This is simply a physical way of acknowledging God and expressing our feelings of devotion before him. In a similar way, the ancients would "fall on their faces" in the presence of the holiness of God. Bowing is a simple way of saying "thank you" when the ministers at the altar assist one another in the conduct of the Eucharist. It saves speaking, and so is not distracting to others.

Genuflecting is a more profound way of bowing. It consists in dropping momentarily to one knee. Its origins go back to the Byzantine court ceremony; one bowed before the emperor's throne when he was absent, but genuflected when he was present. Similarly, when the Blessed Sacrament is present on the altar (or reserved in a tabernacle or aumbry), it is customary to genuflect as a sign of recognition and devotion.

Crossing is done either by a priest, as he makes the sign of the cross over the congregation, or by ourselves. In the former case, it is a symbol of God's grace being dispensed and conveyed by the priest while he is giving absolution (to a single person or the congregation) or pronouncing a blessing. We may also make the sign of the cross at these points to indicate our reception of the grace which is being conveyed. In the West it is done by moving the right hand, with fingers extended, from the forehead to the chest, and then from the left shoulder to right. Orthodox (Eastern) Christians cross themselves from right to left. Signing oneself is rather like putting a signature in a book; the name signifies the person to whom the book belongs. Similarly, when we sign ourselves with Jesus' signature, we are saying, "I am Christ's." In this way, it becomes a visible act of faith and commitment. These are the customary points at which we sign ourselves during the Eucharist: at the beginning of the Gospel, at the end of the Creed, at the absolution, before receiving the bread and wine, and at the final blessing.

Candles

The main reason for using candles in worship is to provide light. At one time, all services were given by candlelight; the celebration of the liturgy at night or early morning obviously required candles. As is often the case, what began as a necessity gradually became formalized. Patterns of use began to develop. Bigger, more important celebrations demanded more candles; a gathering of 500 people at Easter required more than a daily celebration for half a dozen. So rules emerged: two altar candles for a low and six for a high mass, with special candelabra around the altar. Even when new forms of lighting were developed, the candles and the tradition remained. Candles had come to have symbolic meaning as well as aesthetic appeal, rather like candles on the table when we are having guests to a dinner party. Today in most Anglican Churches, it is customary to have two candles at the altar during the liturgy; in some churches there are six during the chief Sunday Eucharist. Others are often lit around the altar, especially on festivals. In addition, candle-bearers (or acolytes) are frequently used to lead the clergy in procession.

Church's Year — Colours

The liturgical colours are a device to highlight the differing seasons of the church year. (The latter does not correspond to the calendar year but starts with the season of Advent, at the beginning of December.) The idea of the church's year is that it gives us an annual cycle, during which we are able to remember and celebrate the great saving events of our faith. It begins with the anticipation of our Lord's coming, and ends with a long season in which we reflect upon God's past and present work through his Holy Spirit. Here is the pattern.

Advent	December	Anticipation of Christ's coming.
Christmas	December 25	Celebration of Christ's birth.
Epiphany	January 6	The manifestation or "revealing" of Christ's divine nature: his baptism.
Lent	February–March (approx.)	Penitential season, originally a preparation time for baptismal candidates; now a time of reflection on human sin and God's love and forgiveness. Lent begins with Ash Wednesday, a day when foreheads are marked with an ash cross, as a reminder of our human mortality.
Passiontide and Holy Week	Preceding Easter	Concentrated attention upon Jesus' passion (suffering) and crucifixion.
Easter	March or April	Christ's Resurrection from the dead; the major Christian festival.

Ascensiontide	Usually in May	Christ's Ascension, marking the close of his visible earthly ministry.
Pentecost	May or June	The pouring out of the Holy Spirit upon the church.

The rest of the year is an extension of Pentecost, emphasizing the life of Christ now active through the Holy Spirit in the church. (In the Prayer Book, Pentecost is followed by the commemoration of the Holy Trinity, a season which extends until Advent. However, this has been superseded in all contemporary prayer books by a reversion to the earlier practice of keeping Pentecost as the final season.)

The church's year is thus securely based on the great drama of what God has done and is doing to save mankind. Part of our celebration of this drama includes a rich pattern of special holy days, commemorating lesser events in the life of our Lord and some of the many saints in his church. These will be found listed on pages ix to xii of the Prayer Book.

All of these seasons and commemorations are marked by four liturgical colours, which clothe both the church and its ministers. Each colour has its special meaning.

White (or Gold):	Festive occasions — Christmas, Easter, Saints' Days in general, baptisms, and weddings.
Purple (or violet):	Generally denotes solemnity and penitence. This is worn in Advent and Lent, and is used for funerals and the hearing of confessions.
Red:	Denotes both the fire of the Holy Spirit and the blood of the martyrs. Thus it is worn on festivals of the Holy Spirit, when the Holy Spirit is being specially invoked (for example, ordinations), or on the commemoration of martyrs.
Green:	The colour of life. It is worn throughout the long season of Pentecost (although not the festival itself), to denote the living nature of the church.

In addition to these four chief colours, rose or blue are sometimes worn at festivals of the Blessed Virgin Mary.

Incense

Incense comes in the form of crystals, which give a pungent but sweet-smelling smoke when placed on glowing charcoal. The incense and charcoal are placed in a metal cup called a thurible which is swung by a thurifer. Its use is now largely aesthetic and symbolic, the smoke representing the prayers of the people ascending to God.

Incense was the ancient equivalent of the common household deodorant! It was impossible to get rid of odours, so people did the next best thing; they introduced other, sweet-smelling ones. Incense was one of the most expensive of these and was widely used in religious ceremonies, notably in the Jewish temple. (We recall that incense was one the precious gifts offered by the wise men at the birth of Jesus.) Inevitably, it came to be adopted in the Christian church, and it continues to be used in all but those of the Protestant tradition. Anglican Churches of a more Catholic tradition burn it during the Eucharist and on other festal occasions.

Music

From the earliest times, Christian worship, and especially the liturgy, has been sung. Saint Paul's "Psalms, hymns, and spiritual songs" (Ephesians 5.19) almost certainly refer to specific kinds of singing which had their roots in the old Jewish traditional forms of worship. Today in the Sunday liturgy, certain parts of the Eucharist continue to be sung (Kyrie, Gloria in Excelsis, Creed, "Lift up your hearts, etc. . .", Holy, Holy, Holy Lord, O Lamb of God . . .) as well as hymns of much later composition. The chanting of psalms originated in the Jewish synagogue. The oldest surviving chants are Gregorian Chant, or Plainsong, used chiefly in Roman, but also in some Anglican, Churches. This goes back some 1300 years to the time when Pope Gregory the Great carried out his great campaign of unification of the Western church. At the time of the Reformation, the Church of England developed "Anglican Chant" based on a more modern but less free-flowing style of music. This remains predominantly an Anglican form. In our own century, another style was developed by Gelineau in France, in order to sing the psalms in the vernacular.

The offices of matins and evensong, as the latter name

implies, are designed to be sung whenever possible; this means not just the psalms and hymns but the office itself. The Anglican Church is particularly fortunate in having compiled these offices at a period of intense musical creativity, so that we have a number of very beautiful traditional settings.

The Building

We all know what a pulpit and altar are, but there are some other names we might not be so sure about. The *sanctuary* is the area immediately around the altar, usually enclosed by the communion rails. The *chancel* (sometimes called the choir) is the part which the choir and clergy usually occupy. The *nave* is where the people sit, derived from the Latin word *navis*, meaning the hull of a ship.

In many churches some of the consecrated bread is reserved after Communion, so that it can be taken to the sick. By church regulations, it has to be reserved in a special safe called a *tabernacle* or *aumbry*. A tabernacle is placed directly on or behind the altar, usually in a side chapel. An aumbry refers to a safe which is actually built into the wall. In both cases the presence of the reserved sacrament is usually indicated by a burning white light, hung above or in front of it.

Vestments

The special robes worn by a priest are of two kinds: vestments worn at the Eucharist and those for matins and evensong (usually called choir habit). The first are derived from those worn by Roman gentlemen in the second century A.D. Because of their beauty and the sense of history which they convey, they have been worn consistently at the Eucharist ever since. These vestments consist of the:

Amice — a decorated hood which hangs down at the back like a collar.

Alb — the long, white garment similar to the Roman toga, with a girdle around the waist.

Stole — literally a scarf, but now stylized and decorated at the ends. It is worn hanging straight down by a bishop, crossed by a priest, and at the side to denote a deacon.

Maniple — originally a handkerchief, now a decorated length of fabric worn over the left wrist (now largely obsolete).

Chasuble— a large, coloured garment, almost circular in shape, worn over the top (the word means a "little tent").

There is usually a set of these vestments in each liturgical colour. Today styles are changing, and a new garment, the "cassock-alb," is often worn, combining the old cassock, alb, and amice in a single garment.

The cassock is simply a heavy alb, traditionally (but no longer) worn as the everyday garment of the priest. The eucharistic vestments were then put on over the top.

For the choir habit, a shorter form of alb called a *surplice* is worn over a cassock — or an even shorter one of hip length, called a *cotta*. Over this is worn a black scarf (sometimes called a preaching scarf or tippet) and the academic hood denoting the priest's university. The relevance of the last item is clearly to the role of the priest as teacher.

The Virgin Mary and the Saints

What do Anglicans believe about saints and the Virgin Mary? The answer is really very simple. We believe that there are some who, in the past, have been so transformed by the Spirit of God that they stand in a class by themselves. We include in this number the apostles of Christ, men of immense stature such as Peter and Paul, martyrs like Stephen, great and holy leaders like Saint John Chrysostom and Saint Francis of Assisi, wise leaders such as Thomas Aquinas and Saint Benedict, men and women of great prayer such as Saint Bernard and Saint Teresa of Avila, and people of our own age, Dietrich Bonhoeffer and Martin Luther King, for example. Such people, we believe, are not only great heroes of the past, but are specially close to God right now. They are part of the "company of heaven," with whom we join in praise every time we celebrate the Eucharist. We commemorate them on their anniversaries year by year, and many people ask for their prayers, believing that, just as we say to each other here and now "please pray for me," so we can ask the saints to do the same.

The Blessed Virgin Mary is the most honoured of all the saints because, as the Council of Chalcedon put it, she is the "bearer of God." She is commemorated no less than five times a year in the church's calendar, and more parish churches are dedicated in her name than in that of any other saint. But Mary is not God, and although she figured prominently in his redemptive purpose, she is not his mediator: this title belongs to Jesus alone. So Mary is venerated as the most loved and greatest of saints and shares in our praise as we commemorate the life of her son.

Notes

1 *Book of Common Prayer* (BCP), page 535.

2 see Revelation 5.13, 7.10 ff, 15.4, and Ephesians 3.20 for examples.

3 Morton Kelsey, *The Other Side of Silence* (London, England: SPCK, 1977).

4 Ian Stuchbery, *Growing in Christ* (Toronto: Anglican Book Centre, 1978).

5 BCP, page 550.

6 BCP, page 535.

7 Stuchbery, *Growing*.

8 Dom Gregory Dix, *The Shape of the Liturgy* (London, England: A & C Black), page 744.

9 P.O. Butterfield, *How to Make Your Confession* (London, England: SPCK, 1952)

10 For a complete account of the place of healing in the life of the church from the New Testament until the present day, see Morton Kelsey, *Healing and Christianity* (New York: Harper and Row, 1976).

11 BCP, pages 638–667.

12 Mark Gibbs, *God's Frozen People* (Glasgow: Fontana, 1971).

13 Michael Harper, *Let My People Grow* (Plainfield: Logos, 1977).

14 For the story of Mother Terese and her dedicated work for the poor of Calcutta, see Malcolm Muggeridge, *Something Beautiful for God* (Glasgow: Fontana, 1971).

15 It is interesting to note that, far from challenging the historical accuracy of much biblical material recording these early years, the study of archaeology has increasingly confirmed its general veracity. See, for example, W.F. Albright, *The Archaeology of Palestine* (Magnolia: Peter Smith).

16 It is quite possible, for example, that we have two accounts of the same event in the stories of the feeding of the crowd in Matthew 14.13 ff and 15.32 ff.

17 Of Mark 8.27 ff and Matthew 16.13 ff where, in Matthew's version, the words "Son of the living God" have been added.

18 An extremely useful book, which takes us back to the probable original forms and meaning of the parables, is Joachim Jeremias, *The Parables of Jesus* (New York: Scriveners, 1971) now abridged as a paperback.

19 Based upon a reconstruction by Canon B.H. Streeter in *The Four Gospels* (Macmillan, 1924), a study which still remains a classic in the field.

20 Reproduced from the article by F.R. Bruce in Peake, *Commentary on the Bible* (Nashville: Nelson, 1962), page 930.

21 Peter, as an orthodox Jew, believed that it was wrong to eat with a non-Jew. Until this barrier had been broken down, there could be no entry for the non-Jew into the Christian church. In this story (Chapter 10), Peter is persuaded that the barrier is down, that the Christian Gospel is for all people.

22 Correspondence between Pliny, governor of the Province of Bithynia, and the Emperor Trajan, quoted in H. Bettenson, *Early Christian Fathers* (Oxford University Press, 1956).

23 Ibid, pages 56–68.

24 Ibid, page 85.

25 This split between the Eastern and Western churches should not be interpreted purely in terms of a power struggle between two rival jurisdictions. Doctrinal issues were also involved in the quarrel, and the two had long since failed to listen to each other well before 1054.

Bibliography

The following books may be useful for those who wish to go more deeply into the many subjects covered by this book. Most of them are available in paperback editions; others may be borrowed from a library or, more probably, from a local clergyman.

The Bible
The following are three sets of commentaries on the books of the Bible. All are good, but they can be compared to find out which best suit the needs of the reader.

The Cambridge Bible Commentary (Old Testament). New York: Cambridge University Press, 1975.

The Abingdon Bible Commentary (Whole Bible). Garden City: Doubleday, 1975.

The Daily Bible Study (New Testament) by William Barclay. Burlington: Welch, 1975.

Albright, Wm.F. *The Archaeology of Palestine.* Pelican Books: Peter Smith.
How archaelogy has shed light upon the story of the Jewish people and their faith until the time of Christ.

Hunter, A.M. *The New Testament for Today.* Edinburgh: St. Andrew's Press, 1974.
A short introduction to the New Testament.

Jeremias, J. *Rediscovering the Parables.* London, England: SCM, 1978.
Fascinating study, helping us to discover what the parables meant in their original setting.

Morison, Frank. *Who Moved the Stone?* London, England: Faber, 1968.
A "whodunnit" approach to the question of the historical resurrection by one who began the book as an agnostic and ended it a believer.

Robinson, J.A.T. *Can we Trust the New Testament?* Oxford: Mowbray, 1977.
Thoughtful defence by a theologian of the New Testament in the light of contemporary scholarship.

Stacey, David. *Interpreting the Bible.* London, England: Sheldon Press, 1976.
Helpful in understanding how to interpret the Bible as the Word of God and yet in the light of critical study.

The Church

Boor, Harry R. *A Short History of the English Church.* Grand Rapids: Eerdmans, 1976.
A basic introduction to the story of the English Church.

Carrington, Philip. *The Anglican Church in Canada.* London, England: Mowbray, 1978.
Worth digging out of a library to discover the story of the Anglican Church in Canada from its beginnings.

Dickens, A.G. *The English Reformation.* New York: Schocken, 1978.
What happened to the Church in England at the time of the Reformation.

Marty, E. Martin. *A Short History of Christianity.* Utica: Meridian, 1959.
A good introductory survey of the rise and development of Christianity from the times of the New Testament.

Moorman, J.R.H. *A History of the Church in England.* London, England: A&C Black, 1976.
This remains a classic history of the English Church; readable and scholarly.

Neil, Stephen. *Anglicanism.* Oxford, Mowbrays, 1978.
A survey of historical and contemporary Anglicanism, set within the broader context of the catholic Church.

Especially good is the Pelican History of the Christian Church, published by Penguin Books. This is a series of six paperback volumes by leading Church historians. Reasonably priced, scholarly, and readable.

Introduction to Theology

Barclay, Wm. *A Plain Man Looks at the Apostles Creed.* London, England: Fontana: 1967.

Readable, paperback introduction to the basic beliefs of the Creed.

Edwards, David L. *The Last Things Now*. London, England, SCM, 1969.
A reflection on the meaning of such things as the Second Coming and the end of the world.

Lewis, C.S.: *Mere Christianity*. New York: Macmillan, 1960.
This remains a classic in helping us to grasp ''what the Christian faith is really all about.''

Lewis, C.S. *Miracles*. London, England: Fontana, 1960.
A look at miracles, by one who really believes in them.

Ramsey, Michael. *Holy Spirit*. London, England, SPCK, 1971.
The former Archbishop of Canterbury writes simply of the person and work of the Holy Spirit.

Prayer and Spiritual Growth

Bennett, Dennis. *Nine O'Clock in the Morning*. Sussex: Coverdale, 1974.
A personal testimony to the renewing power of the Holy Spirit by a priest whose personal ministry was transformed.

Bennett, Dennis. *The Holy Spirit and You*. Sussex: Coverdale, 1974.
Practical and reflective guide as to how our personal lives can be renewed by the Holy Spirit.

Bloom, Anthony. *Beginning to Pray*. New York: Paulist Press, 1971.
Short book by the Russian Archbishop on how to begin to pray; a good introduction by a well known spiritual writer.

Ellul, Jacques. *Prayer and Modern Man*. New York: Seabury, 1973.
Helpful guide in relating the practice of prayer to today's secular world.

Fuller, R.H. *The Foundations of New Testament Christology*. London, England: Fontana, 1965
How the first Christian witness began to answer the question, ''Just Who was Jesus?''

Kelsey, Morton. *The Other Side of Silence*. New York: Paulist Press, 1976.
Perceptive and practical introduction to meditation, what it is and how to set about it: stresses importance of dreams.

Leech, Kenneth. Soul Friend. London, England: Sheldon Press, 1977.
Excellent guide to spiritual growth in today's world by a perceptive Anglican priest.

Lewis, C.S. *The Screwtape Letters.* London, England: Collins, 1979.
Humorous classic on how the devil infiltrates into and manipulates our lives. Even if you don't believe in a personal devil, the message is still relevant.

Merton, Thomas. *New Seeds of Contemplation.* New York: New Directions, 1972.
One of the many books on prayer by one one of today's most widely read spiritual writers.

Pulkingham, W. Graham. *Gathered for Power.* London, England, Hodder & Staughten, 1974.
The story of what can happen when a parish truly opens itself to God. The author is rector of the Church of the Redeemer in Houston, and he writes of his own parish.

The Sacraments

Kelsey, Morton. *Healing and Christianity.* New York: Harper & Row, 1976.
Definitive study of the place of healing in the Christian church from the New Testament until today.

MacNutt, Francis. *Healing.* Notre Dame: Ave Maria Press, 1974.
_____ *The Power to Heal.* Bantam, 1974.
Readable and informative books written by a priest who has been at the heart of the renewal of healing through prayer in the contemporary church.

Butterfield, Peter D. *How to Make Your Confession.* London, England: SPCK, 1952.
Practical booklet designed to explain what the sacrament of absolution is all about and how to set about making one's confession.

There have been a large number of books in recent years written on the subjects of Christian Initiation (Baptism and Confirmation) and the Eucharist. Many of these have been in the form of short books or booklets. This reflects the great amount of attention which has focused upon these particular sacraments from both the theological and the pastoral perspectives. For further reading I would suggest:

a the continuing studies in the Canadian Anglican Liturgical Series published by the Anglican Book Centre;

b a similar series produced by the Joint Liturgical Group in England published by SPCK.

Ministry and Social Responsibility

Davies, Horton. *Christian Deviations*. London, England: SCM, 1974.

An informative look at the growing number of non-Christian sects today, from Jehovah's Witnesses to the Church of Scientology.

George, Susan. *How the Other Half Dies*. London, England: Penguin, 1976.

An informative and challenging book on how it is that more than half the world is hungry in an increasingly affluent world.

Harper, Michael. *Let My People Grow*. London, England: Hodder & Staughton

How Christians can be released for ministry in the Body of Christ. Important in its implications for parish renewal.

Simon, Arthur: *Bread for My People*. New York: Paulist, 1974.

The role of Christians in a hungry world.

Temple, William. *Christianity and the Social Order*. London, England: SPCK, 1976.

This remains as fresh a statement of the relationship between religion and politics as when it was first written by the then Archbishop of Canterbury forty years ago. Perceptive and readable.

Watson, David. *I Believe in Evangelism*. London, England: Hodder & Staughton, 1976.

A powerful, thoughtful, and contemporary call to evangelism by one of today's most effective English evangelists.

General

The Church's Teaching Series Toronto: Anglican Book Centre, 1979.

An excellent follow-up to this book.